"DOE[S] DI[D] MAKE ME LOOK FAT?"

A MAN'S GUIDE
TO THE LOADED QUESTIONS WOMEN ASK

Tyndale House Publishers, Inc.
Carol Stream, Illinois

STEPHEN JAMES
DAVID THOMAS

Visit Tyndale's exciting Web site at www.tyndale.com

"Does This Dress Make Me Look Fat?" A Man's Guide to the Loaded Questions Women Ask

Designed by Jacqueline L. Noe

Edited by Dave Lindstedt

Published in association with the literary agency of Baugher & Co., 611 Eastcastle Court, Franklin, TN 37069.

Library of Congress Cataloging-in-Publication Data

James, Stephen.
  Does this dress make me look fat? : a man's guide to the loaded questions women ask / Stephen James and David Thomas.
      p. cm.
  Includes bibliographical references.
  ISBN-13: 978-1-4143-1302-3 (sc)
  ISBN-10: 1-4143-1302-0 (sc)
  1. Man-woman relationships—Religious aspects—Christianity. 2. Marriage—Religious apsects—Christianity. 3. Women—Psychology. I. Thomas, David. II. Title
  BT705.8.J36 2007
  284.8'4—dc22   2006037854

Printed in the United States of America

13   12   11   10   09   08   07
7   6   5   4   3   2   1

CONTENTS

THESE BOOKS MADE US *LAUGH!*

More than that, they gave us so much insight into the way the other thinks and how we could possibly communicate better.

Each book is an easy, fun read that you'll tell your friends about.

SINGER/SONGWRITER **CINDY MORGAN** AND HUSBAND, AUTHOR **SIGMUND BROUWER**

ACKNOWLEDGMENTS

WRITING, THOUGH A romantic notion, always requires much more effort than one ever really anticipates. It's kind of like dating. At the outset, you have this energy and chemistry and everything is so easy, fun, and intoxicating. Over time, however, as the infatuation fades, things progressively grow more serious. You have to make a decision to commit to the process and submit to the hard and rewarding work of making it the best that it can be. If you don't, it is sure to all fall apart.

In that way, we've been burning the candle at both ends as we simultaneously wrote two books, *"Does This Dress Make Me Look Fat?"* and *"Yup." "Nope." "Maybe."* Initially, it was exciting—like dating two women at the same time. Then it got hard—like dating two women at the same time. Then it got really, really hard—like getting caught dating two women at the same time. By the end, we were spent.

Amazingly, however, with the help of a really good team (our own "dysfunctional family"), it all turned out well in the end.

Thanks to the entire crew at Tyndale for their encouragement, professionalism, and effort. Working with you all is nothing short of fantastic. Thanks especially to Ken Petersen and Carol Traver for investing deeply in two goobers from Tennessee and believing that depth and humor aren't mutually exclusive. Deep gratitude is also owed to Dave Lindstedt, our fearless editor, whose firm but gentle hand made everything you read . . . well, readable.

We must also thank our remarkable agent, Matt Baugher. Thanks for representing us so well, for being so diplomatic, and for rounding off a lot of our rough edges. It is an honor to know you and to work alongside you.

Heather and Connie, our wonderful wives. At times you must have felt cheated on when it came to this process, and your full support of the whole writing thing is humbling. There really aren't words to acknowledge your sacrifice—and we don't even pretend to understand.

We are continuously awed by God's grace and his profound sense of humor. That he would entrust us with the opportunity to write of his mystery and magnificence is baffling and humbling. If you discover anything more of his love and mercy in these pages, it is indeed a miracle.

Stephen and David

INTRODUCTION

WHEN I (STEPHEN) was a kid, Friday night was often a night when my mom, dad, sister, and I would pile into the car and go out to eat. Some Fridays, we would get pizza; other times, we would pick up burgers; but most often we would enact a crazy merry-go-round-like ritual that I have since dubbed The Search.

On those nights, my sister and I would listen from the back seat as my parents volleyed suggestions about where we were going to dine. It usually started with my father throwing out an idea or two (or three, or four, or fifty) and my mother deflecting, rejecting, negotiating, or ignoring his proposals. Periodically, either my sister or I would blurt out an option to help keep up the momentum. It went something like this:

Dad: Where would you like to eat tonight?

Mom: What were *you* thinking?

Dad: Anywhere, really. I don't care.

Mom: It doesn't really matter to me. What do you kids want?

Kids: What about pizza?

Dad: Well, I'll be happy wherever we go.

Depending on the time, my father's appetite, and my mother's mood, this part of the conversation—let's call it The Warm Up—could last a few exchanges or extend to several minutes; but, inevitably, my father would start the ball rolling by suggesting several possibilities.

Dad: How about Mexican?

He didn't always lead off with Mexican. Sometimes, it would be Italian, or Chinese, or on a rare occasion German, but he usually started by proposing some sort of ethnic cuisine.

Mom: I don't know. That sounds awfully spicy . . .

. . . or heavy, or salty, or whatever, depending on the perceived shortcomings of the food Dad had suggested. After a few circles of the culinary world, Dad would typically shift tactics and go with some regional options.

Dad: Catfish would be good. How about that?

Mom: Too fried and greasy.

Dad: What about barbecue?

Mom: We had that last week.

Dad: What about Tex-Mex?

Mom: I said I didn't want Mexican.

At this point, the tension began to build between them. Remember, this all took place *while* we were driving around . . . and around . . . and around, passing restaurant after restaurant after restaurant, and my sister and I were growing hungrier and hungrier and hungrier. Then, my dad started listing restaurants by how often we ate there.

Dad: How about we go to Ruby Tuesday's? That's always good.

Mom: I feel like we eat there all the time.

Dad: Then how about we go to that new place out by the mall?

Mom: I heard it wasn't so good.

Dad: How about Cracker Barrel then? We haven't been there in a while.

Mom: It takes too long.

Dad: Well, what about Chili's?

Mom: How many times do I have to tell you, I don't want Mexican?

On and on this would go, mile after mile, until—predictably—we would arrive at the same two sentences . . .

Dad: Well, where *do* you want to eat?

Mom: How about somewhere with a salad bar?

Now, I knew what my dad was thinking, because my sister and I were thinking the same thing: *Why didn't you just say* salad bar *from the beginning?*

Dad: You can get a salad anywhere!

Mom: But not everywhere has a *good* salad.

So, we would pull into one of the few places that had a "good" salad, but by that late hour the wait to get a table was so long that we would—as you might expect—grab a pizza or some burgers and go home.

SOMETHING SO SIMPLE . . . NOT!

I never thought much about what I had witnessed from the back seat until one weekend when I was on a date with Heather before we got married, and we reenacted the same scene. I asked her what I thought was a straightforward question: "Where do you want to eat?"

Before I knew it—wham, bam, thank you ma'am—we were tangled up in conflict. When it was over, I was confused, angry, and still hungry, though eventually we did find someplace to eat. (I don't remember where.)

When I got home that night, after dropping Heather off, I started thinking: *Where did I go wrong? What did I say? What didn't I say? What could I have said? Why are women the way they are? What do they really want? Why do they do the things they do?*

What man or woman can't share a similar story where the guy thought things were pretty clear and direct, and the woman was coming from an entirely different perspective? You see, what is at play is far more complex than where to go for dinner. What drives the conversation is two people with vastly different agendas. The man wants a decision made and a plan in place. The woman, on the other hand, wants conversation and dialogue and a union of opinion. It is here, at the convergence of these two positions, that men and women often find themselves wanting different things from the same moment.

At some point, every man has walked through the minefield of a woman's questions. He can usually smell the danger, but he often underestimates the explosive potential of a wrong answer. Many a man knows all too well the folly of blindly answering his girlfriend's or wife's questions. But few men (or women, for that matter) ever stop to think about what is really being asked. At its core, this book is about those questions, questions like these:

- "Does this dress make me look fat?"
- "Do you notice anything different about the house?"
- "Do you think that woman is pretty?"
- "What are you thinking about?"
- "Am I like my mother?"
- "Are you as happy as I am?"
- "Is there anything you don't like about me?"

IF YOU REALLY LISTEN . . .

Here is the thing about questions: They expose more about the asker than they do about the one being asked. If you pay attention, you will see that a woman's questions point directly to some of her deepest longings. They also reveal some of what she desires most from a man. Just as we set out to decode *manspeak* in the companion volume to this book *("Yup." "Nope." "Maybe."),* here we're attempting to unveil the authentic heart of women by shedding some light on the "loaded" questions they ask men. We hope that men and women can move beyond the question, Why are women the way they are? to see the authentic female heart. When men and women are more aware, two things can happen: (1) Men can give better answers, and (2) women can ask better questions. This book, as honestly as possible, examines and explains the themes behind the questions and what the questions reveal about the women who ask them and the men who are confused by them.

As therapists with thousands of combined hours counseling men, women, and couples about the dynamics of relationship, and as husbands each with more than a decade of marriage to draw upon, we want to offer insight as to why women and men do what they do. For sure, men and women share a lot in common. Chemically and elementally, we are identical. Physiologically and biologically, our bodies function similarly. Spiritually, we both are created to reflect the image of God, and we simultaneously struggle with our lack of virtue. On an emotional level, men and women feel, need, desire, long, and hope. And though we are very alike, it's the differences that often make life most interesting, fulfilling, and frustrating and give us the most insight into who we are and who we are made to be. As relational beings, much of the tension, joy, and ambiguity of life is tied to our sexuality, and that's what this book is about: exploring the differences between women and men, entering the mysterious space that separates the sexes, and highlighting how God marks us for glory through our gender.

Perhaps a good picture that underlines the differences between men and women and how they relate occurred some time ago when I (Stephen) was having coffee with a friend. This guy is quite a bit older and has been married for more than thirty years. We were discussing the complexity of marriage and how women and men seem to be so different at times.

I asked my friend, "You've been married a long time. Surely you know why men and women are so apt for conflict." He reclined back in his chair and thought for a long moment, staring at the ceiling. Then he slowly leaned forward with his eyes narrowed to almost slits, dramatically glanced around as if to make sure no one was listening, and then in a low voice said, "When four or more men get together, they talk about sports. When four or more women get together, they talk about men. If you understand that, you understand everything."

That about says it.

1
"DOES THIS DRESS MAKE ME LOOK FAT?"

YOU COULDN'T TELL in a million years by how I (Stephen) dress now, but back in the day, I was stylish. Whatever the latest fashion, I was sure to be in vogue. To vandalize a classic country-and-western song, I was Metro when Metro wasn't cool. Or to put it more bluntly: I was a shallow, self-absorbed pretty boy.

To support my clothes habit, at various times I worked at an assortment of clothing stores: Eddie Bauer, Britches, Abercrombie & Fitch (before it catered to teen porn-star-wannabes), a couple different department stores, and even a local boutique. Most of the stores were trendy, and almost all carried women's and men's items.

Throughout the three or four years that I hawked clothes, I got to meet a variety of people: rich and poor; tall and short; thin and fat; urban and suburban; young and old. All kinds of people crossed my path. It was my job to assist them in finding whatever they needed in order to look however they wanted.

I distinctly remember a time right before Christmas. It was a weekend and the store was really crowded, full of holiday shoppers who were scrambling to find the presents they still needed. That day, I was working the registers beside a coworker. The line was long, and despite our best efforts, things were moving rather slowly. One customer in particular caught my attention. She was a thirtysomething professional who seemed rather anxious that the line was taking so long. I saw her head bobbing back and forth, her toe tapping, as she huffed and puffed and exhaled loudly enough for me to hear her above the commotion of the store from her position in line.

As she gradually made her way up in line, I noticed that she was pregnant. Not a little pregnant, but swallowed-a-beach-ball pregnant. But what was even more noticeable than her extra-large, I'm-about-to-give-birth belly was that she was extremely angry. I made eye contact with her and offered a conciliatory smile in an effort to communicate that I understood that this was taking longer than it should, and if she could just wait another moment or two, I'd be able to help her. My grin had zero effect on her. In response she rolled her eyes so dramatically that I thought for a second she might be having some kind of labor-related convulsion.

That's when the register ran out of tape. My heart raced, knowing that this would slow the line down all the more. I scrambled around the counter for another roll of tape and fumbled to install it into the register. At this point, Psycho Pregnant Lady could not contain herself. She let loose a rant of curse words that would make a Mafia crime boss go red in the face. I didn't know that there were that many ways to defame the name of God. I even remember her slandering the Republican party somewhere in there. It's as if she was going for some kind of Guinness record for cursing. One mother awkwardly scurried to cover her three children's ears but did not have enough hands to get the job done. Next to her in line was a massive bodybuilder guy (he must have been 6'5", 280 pounds), who slowly backed away from the scene and just dropped the clothes he was planning to purchase.

To say that it was a scene would be an understatement. It was embarrassing for everyone around. People turned and looked at her with shock and fear. Passersby in the mall slowed and gawked—like people driving past a traffic accident. It was indeed an implausible prospect: this professional, attractive, pregnant woman cursing like an R-rated movie.

As Psycho Pregnant Lady began to slow her verbal assault on the store, on me, and on all things holy, I began to realize that everyone else in the vicinity directed their gaze toward me, the lowly, well-groomed cashier. They were wondering, like I was, how in the world I was going to respond. Shell-shocked, I just stood openmouthed for a few seconds, searching for something to say. The only thing that came to my mind was, "You seem really angry." Now even more enraged, Psycho Pregnant Lady stormed out of the store, vowing never to return.

Not every encounter was this violent, but some were even more bizarre. There was the time that a short, slender, polyester-wearing gentleman came to buy some socks, but insisted on measuring each sock before he tried them on. Then there was the lady who came in almost every Friday and purchased several new outfits, only to return them all on Sunday afternoon. Like I said, I got to meet a lot of different kinds of people.

SKINNY-DIPPING

It wasn't long into my run as a retail sales associate that I noticed a rather obvious difference in how men and women shop for clothes. The men tended to move directly and single-mindedly toward the section of the store where they needed to go, whether they were shopping for pants or shoes or shirts.

The women, on the other hand, meandered around the store, touching and examining various articles: holding one up; sizing it in their mind; maybe holding it up again in front of the mirror; then putting it down and moving along to the next rack, or back to the last rack, or to a rack on the other side of the store. Women also had multiple options in multiple cuts, shapes, and sizes that pushed this way, pulled that way, fit here, tugged there.

One area where I saw a real difference was when it came to looking for a new bathing suit. For example, guys (if they even opted for actual swim trunks and not just an old pair of shorts), might riffle through a rack of trunks for a few minutes, pick out a style they like, find their size, and purchase it. We're talking fifteen minutes max. Women, on the other hand, entered this moment with much more angst. As my mother-in-law said the other day, if a woman wants to get depressed, all she has to do is go shopping for bathing suits.

Women typically begin preparing for this event a few days in advance. They'll do things like cut back on calories and make an extra trip to the gym. It's rare to see a woman shop for a bathing suit alone. Usually, she'll bring along a girlfriend or two for moral support. And, unlike men, women try on multiple suits in front of multiple full-length mirrors—the kind that show every body part from multiple angles. Now, for sure, there are some women who could enter this scene without self-contempt, but many more women find the ordeal of shopping for a new bathing suit a dreadful experience.

BIG MONEY AND BIG RESPONSIBILITY

According to the U.S. Food and Drug Administration, approximately 50 million Americans will go on diets in the coming year, spending "an estimated $30 billion a year on all types of diet programs and products, including diet foods and drinks."[1] The weight-loss industry is an entity in itself.

Why would 50 million people spend $30 billion dollars on trying to lose weight? The money we spend on weight loss in this country could eliminate famine in several third-world countries. The money we spend on trying *not* to eat could put food on the table for millions of starving people across the world. So why do we do it? We do it for a number of different reasons. One of those reasons, at least for women, is that they want to be beautiful. In our culture, being thin equates to being beautiful. Women are bombarded every day with this perception.

IS BEAUTY REALLY ONLY SKIN DEEP?

Does this dress make me look fat? Every woman will speak those words at one time or another, either aloud or in her own head. And there will be a hundred moments throughout her life that will define how she experiences that question and what she believes to be true about herself.

Angela Thomas in her excellent and engaging book *Do You Think I'm Beautiful?* writes extensively about this theme and what is at the core of femininity. She says, "Every woman longs to know from the deepest place of her heart, 'Oh, God, do you think I'm beautiful?'"[2] Sadly, these women often find themselves in lives filled with duty, difficulty, and demands. What's even more unfortunate is that many Christian women are struggling under the weight of the pressure to be the perfectly patient mother and perfectly submissive wife.

The women who are meant to be living the most free, the Christians, are often the most bound and ashamed. Too many women have lost their sense of personal beauty (a beauty that is both inward and outward). But it goes deeper than a sense of personal beauty. Perhaps a better term would be *loveliness*.

GLASS SLIPPER, ANYONE?

So what's all this about? It all has to do with Julia Roberts—kind of. One of the most popular films of the early '90s was *Pretty Woman*, starring Julia Roberts and Richard Gere. Box office receipts for *Pretty Woman* exceeded $175 million, making it one of the most successful romantic comedies of all time.[3] On the surface, this story is about a prostitute who finds true love with one of her johns. At its core, however, it's about so much more. Why was *Pretty Woman* such a popular movie? What about the movie stirred the hearts of women? For the answer, we only have to listen to the main character, Vivian Ward (played by Roberts), who says it well: "I want the fairy tale."

Pretty Woman is essentially a retelling of Cinderella—one of the most recognized stories around the world. The earliest recorded version of the tale comes from China, and was written in the middle of the tenth century. Literary scholars think that there are as many as 1,500 versions of the Cinderella tale, if you include all the picture books, musicals, and theatrical interpretations. While being dubbed "sexist" and "demeaning" by many feminist critics, Cinderella obviously has elements that rouse the feminine soul.

Our school-age daughters love the story of Cinderella. My (Stephen's) daughter has Cinderella toothbrushes, books, and movies. From an early age, she was captivated by the classic Disney version. She would watch the movie over and over and over. It got to the point where as parents we would have to limit the number of times she could watch the movie in a month. There were times when she would insist that I pretend to be the prince and she would be Cinderella so we could reenact the royal ball in our living room.

This past weekend, our daughters performed in their first real dance recital. They've been taking ballet together for a couple of years, and in past years they've had "observations." An observation is where all the moms and dads show up with video cameras, the teacher turns on some soft music, and all these little preschool girls start twirling around in circles, bumping into each other and leaping from spot to spot. Some of the girls just stand there and stare. Some tug at tight leotards. While all this twirling, colliding, tugging, and staring is taking place, the adults clap and smile and take a thousand pictures. The girls do their thing, the adults do theirs, and we all call it ballet.

Well, this year was the real deal. Four-hour dress rehearsal, fifty-dollar costumes, hair in a tight bun—the whole nine yards.

They even sent home an instruction page illustrating how to twist the girls' hair into the proper bun.

So, we all filed in and found our seats in the massive auditorium. All the dads were holding bouquets of flowers to give their daughters following the performance; the little brothers of the performers looked bored and restless, and the show hadn't even started yet; there were video cameras mounted on tripods up and down every aisle; and grandparents had traveled from all ends of the country to witness maybe sixty-three seconds of magic.

My (David's) five-year-old daughter had been talking about her performance for about a month prior to this night. Periodically, she talked about the dance, but it was mostly about the costume. Suffice to say, she was extremely excited about the little pale blue tutu she got to wear. I had yet to see the infamous tutu because it's so sacred (and so expensive) that you can't take it home until *after* the performance. (I assumed it stayed encased in glass in the dance school vault until recital day.) At breakfast the morning of the recital, my daughter asked, "Did you know I get to bring my tutu home tonight?"

"Is tonight the night?" I asked with great excitement, playing dumb for a moment.

"Yes, and did you remember that it's blue and matches the sequined leotard?" she said, just to make certain I'd been paying attention the other *fifty-two* times we'd discussed it.

"Of course I remember. And you can sleep in it tonight if you want to. You know you get to keep it forever," I reminded her.

"Yeah," she said, with an enormous grin of deep satisfaction on her face (the way I always look after the first bite of Ben Jerry's). She glazed over for a moment.

"Sweetheart, I can hardly wait to watch you dance today. Do you know how much I love to watch you doing something that you love that much?" I asked.

"Yeah," she said again. "And tonight I'll be dancing in my real tutu." (She stared into the sky and I could just see the little white cloud above her head with a vision of herself in it.)

A few hours later, she left for the recital with my wife to put on the sacred costume, apply her little stage makeup, and have her picture taken while doing some plié or pirouette. I packed up her brothers and her grandfather, who was visiting from Florida, and off we went.

Within a few minutes after we arrived, the lights dimmed, the director introduced the evening, and then class by class, the dancers took the stage. The preteen girls did hip-hop, because I guess ballet is so not cool when you're twelve, but I think it becomes in vogue again when you turn seventeen (and return to being a normal person). The preteens wore baggy cargo pants and tight shirts and did all these in-your-face moves to loud rap music. The rapper kept yelling, "Yeah boy. Yeah boy." I felt a little violated after their performance (like I needed to smoke a cigarette or pick a fight or something). I was so thankful my daughter is only five and still excited about big fluffy tutus. I'm not quite ready to share my home with weird, moody, sullen, irritable, angry preteens or adolescents. (I need a couple more years to build up to all that fun.)

Once the rapping tweens strutted off the stage, soft music began to play, and we all relaxed again as a parade of blue tutus emerged. They all reached the stage, and it looked like a cotton candy machine had just overheated and blew up. I've never seen so much fluffy blue.

Third in line was my little girl in her magical costume, and she was beaming from ear to ear. Her hair was in a little bun on the top of her head. She took her spot on the front row and began her ballerina moves. Her delicate little frame moved across the stage as she smiled and twirled, lifting her arms, with her tiny hands taking different forms. From time to time, she froze in these little positions with her arms pointing upward and then from side to side. And I started to weep. Then I began to sob uncontrollably.

I wasn't prepared for this moment. The moment when my little girl, whom I love with all of my being, took the stage in all her innocent beauty and danced with such delight. I couldn't stop weeping. Tears just poured down my face. My wife looked at me staring at this little person, who just five years ago was growing inside her womb. She just held my hand, and we tried to take it all in.

I jumped ahead twenty years in my mind and imagined repeating this same kind of moment. I open a door and there stands my little girl in a long, white dress, a veil over her face and flowers in her hand. I'm handing her over to some numbskull, who claims he'll love her for the rest of her life. (My daughter is an artist. She loves to paint and draw. So she'll probably fall in love with some stinkin' musician, who'll be broke for most of his life. They'll live in a run-down apartment with two large, mixed breed dogs, and she'll have to wait tables at night while he plays gigs. *Help!*) On their wedding day, I'll watch her dance in his arms at the close of the evening. She'll smile and twirl, her arms and hands intertwined in his. I am certain I'll just weep. I will probably weep uncontrollably again. And I'll remember when she was this delicate little five-year-old ballerina.

After the performance ended, my wife and I slipped out of the auditorium and through the side door to see the dancers as they exited the building, heading back to their dressing room. I saw Lily from a distance, and she was beaming. She had no idea I was watching her. She looked so full of delight and pleasure. She and her classmates were all giggling and skipping, some of them holding hands. As she neared the sidewalk where we were standing, she saw me, jumped out of line, and came running toward me. She leapt into my arms, and I teared up all over again. I spun her around and kissed her and gave her the big bouquet of pink tulips. She smiled, thanked me, and then I asked her, "Sweetheart, do you know why daddy is crying?" She just stared at my face. "I'm crying because you're so beautiful and it overwhelms me." She continued to just look at me.

"And I'm *so* happy when I watch you dance, because you love it so much, don't you?" She smiled, nodded, and looked overwhelmed by my tears and my words.

"I couldn't take my eyes off you tonight," I said, and she stayed frozen for that moment.

I was unaware at the time, but my wife was taking pictures of the two of us as this exchange played out, and I have a snapshot that I treasure. I believe my daughter was frozen in that moment by my words, because they are the words that her little heart just longed to hear. They are the words that every woman, from the earliest moments of her life, hungers for and craves from the deepest part of her being. It begins with a little girl's desire to hear her dad acknowledge and affirm her beauty—to speak of who she is and how she is made—to speak to the beauty of her design.

At the recital, our daughters got to be Cinderella. The

Cinderella concept tells us a lot about the nature of women. Perhaps one of the clearest scenes about what is happening in the heart of a woman comes with the fairy godmother. It's a familiar scene. The wicked stepmother and stepsisters have left for the ball, and a brokenhearted Cinderella stands alone weeping. From nowhere appears her fairy godmother. With a wave of the wand, Cinderella's tattered old dress is transformed into a beautiful gown. Cinderella is breathtaking. Her beauty is revealed and enhanced. She makes it to the ball and overwhelms Prince Charming with her beauty. She captivates the entire room. There is a night of dancing, a hurried farewell, a desperate search for love, a glass slipper, and a happy ending.

BEAUTY TARNISHED

Do women want to look pretty? Do women care if their butts look big in dresses? Yes, but there is something far deeper stirring in the soul of a woman than the appearance of her derriere. What every woman most struggles with is a sense of shame that exposes that she is broken or ugly on the inside. On some level, every woman wrestles with the question, Am I lovely? Every woman wants to believe she is lovely. That's the real question behind, Do I look fat? Loveliness has beauty in it but goes far past reflecting physical attractiveness. Loveliness speaks of character. Loveliness implies charm, compassion, invitation, tenderness, and allure. Loveliness is the reflection of God's image that is stamped into the heart of every woman. You see, women are designed for more than the drudgery of life. Every woman is marked with the nature of beauty. Women are designed by God to reveal beauty.

Most women grow up with a longing to feel lovely, but deep

in their souls suspect they are not. That is because, tragically, at some point, something happened that attached shame to their femininity. Every woman has experienced shame in terms of her sexuality. Being a woman has caused her to feel powerless, abandoned, or abused. This can come from something as simple as boys getting called on in class far more frequently, or as mischievous as getting their bra straps popped in middle school. But far too often it's much more severe. Here are some of the most heartbreaking statistics:

- Girls are sexually abused about three times more often than boys.[4]
- Approximately one in six American women has been the victim of an attempted or completed rape.[5]
- About 44 percent of rape victims are minors, and 80 percent are under age thirty.[6]

A few years ago, I (Stephen) counseled a professional model. She came to see me because she was growing increasingly depressed and hopeless. This woman was distractingly beautiful. Both men and women noticed her when she walked into a room.

During one of the early counseling sessions, she and I were talking about what might be at the root of her depression. I asked her what she thought about how people see her: "Are you aware of how beautiful other people find you?" She looked at me with anger in her eyes.

"If I hear that I am beautiful one more time . . . !" she threatened.

"One more time what? What might happen?" I asked.

"I don't know. I just feel so ugly on the inside. And so alone." Her anger melted and she began to cry.

"Who told you that you were beautiful?" I gently asked.

As we continued our conversation over the next several appointments, she began to tell me about how her swim coach "touched" her in middle school, how her high school boyfriend "went too far," and how her mother was always critical of her weight. Far too many women have experienced similar events. If a woman is to live without toxic shame, she must come to terms with this heartache and reconcile her identity.

REDEEMING BEAUTY: THE EYE OF THE BEHOLDER

It's Saturday night. A guy shows up at his girlfriend's house to pick her up for a romantic night out. He is right on time, but she is running a few minutes late and is still in jeans and a T-shirt. "I can't decide which dress to wear. Can you help me out? Wait right here. I'll be right back." Before he can even answer, she disappears into the bedroom to change. Moments later she reemerges from the bedroom. "Does this dress make me look fat?"

Is this a loaded question? You bet it is. No matter how he answers it, he will immediately find himself trapped. How does this work? It has as much to do with the nature of the question as it does anything else. Like lawyers, women are experts at posing questions that seem to have no right answer. What's a guy to do?

There's an old joke. You can decide for yourself if it's funny or not. It goes something like this: A woman comes into the room and asks her husband, who is watching television, "Does this dress

14

make me look fat?" The husband pauses for a moment, and then he responds, "No, the dress is fine. It's the pint of ice cream you eat every night that makes you look fat."

Not a great answer. Here are some other incredibly wrong ways to answer the question, Does this dress make me look fat?

- "I guess not. A few extra pounds look good on you."
- "Fat? Compared to whom?"
- "Well, you've been fatter."
- "I don't know. What do you think?"
- "It doesn't matter to me."

The guy doesn't even have to say anything to miss the mark. Hesitating, stuttering, or pausing before answering is equally as tragic. And pretending not to hear the question isn't any better: "I'm sorry, honey. Did you say something?"

Remember, beneath the question, Does this dress make me look fat? a woman is really asking, Am I lovely? What she is looking for is a man who will do three things:

- tell her the truth
- confront her shame
- confirm her loveliness

Any woman who asks this question already has a pretty good idea of the right answer, so if a guy lies, she knows it. Does she look fat? On the surface, this is a yes or no question, and this part of the question must be addressed if the man is to have integrity and authenticity.

And though her butt may look as big as a Clydesdale pony's, it's her shame that the guy is actually dealing with. The question of her heart is, Are you with me for how I look, or do you see something else that keeps you here?

When she asks, "Do I look fat in this dress?" one of two things can happen: Her shame will be exposed or it will be diminished.

He can answer, "No, you look great, and I really like the way the dress shows off your _____ ." (Fill in what you really notice. The blank could be anything as long as it's honest. It could be eyes, skin tone, hair, or another attractive body part.) Keep in mind that, even though he says she looks great, she may not like his answer. If she rejects it, her shame will be exposed, and she will change dresses anyway. If she accepts the answer, her self-contempt will be diminished, and she will be humbled—as long as the guy is telling the truth.

This is where a man can really bless a woman. This is the moment when he can help her grow in maturity, wisdom, and love. This is a moment when he can help her see herself as God sees her. She asks, "Do I look fat in this dress?" He answers, "No, and I really like the way the dress shows off your eyes. Do you want to know what I like more than that?" . . . *Dramatic pause* . . . "How you are so generous with your friends. You care for them so well." This would surprise her. It would speak to her character. She would know that he really notices her.

What if he answers, "Yes, it does make you look fat"? What should a guy do? Duck behind the couch? Run for cover? Get an extra blanket for the doghouse? Quite honestly, there's not a whole lot a man can say after yes that will really matter. She already knows she looks fat and he just confirmed it, and now the shame she felt is out in the open and exposed. But for the heck of it, let's finish the sentence.

So he says, "Yes." There is blessing to be given here too. "Yes, you do look fat in that dress, and I wonder if you already thought that. If you really want my opinion, I like the blue dress you wore last week. You look great in that dress. But you know what I really see when you ask me that?" . . . *Dramatic pause* . . . "I see a woman who hates her body, and it breaks my heart for you. I wish you could see yourself the way God sees you." It takes a good deal of courage to do this. It also takes equal measures of strength and tenderness. And any man that stops at a simple yes (or no for that matter) is not courageous but cruel.

Any guy who can candidly tell a woman she looks fat with gentleness has credibility. He's a man that tells the truth. When a question is answered honestly and the woman is confirmed for who she is by a man who cares for her deeply, it creates a sense of security and wholeness (even if it's an answer she doesn't like hearing). It creates a sense of being known and understood. When a man is committed to telling the truth, confronting shame, and confirming the loveliness of character in a woman, he is doing the work of God. When he dodges the question, he is being a childish coward.

The hope is that the woman, regardless of how she looks, can begin to live more deeply out of her identity in Christ. Her sense of femininity is rooted in being loved, honored, valued, and cherished by another for who she *is,* not for how she looks.

Women are made to reveal beauty. Men are made to view it. This is how beauty can be redeemed. Men are made to delight in the beauty of a woman. But if men only look at the skin, they will miss the depth of loveliness that a woman has to offer. And if women look to men for their definition, they will always be disappointed. True beauty is about a woman's character—about her story—and it always refers to what God has done in her.

Though men don't define a woman's loveliness (God does that), they do have the power to confirm it or tarnish it. So when a woman asks a man, "Do I look fat in this dress?" what she is asking is for confirmation of who she is. Whatever the man's answer, he must address her character, her nature, who she is in God's image, if his answer is to be truthful.

HERE'S THE POINT

The real question behind Do I look fat? is, Am I lovely? Based on what we just told you, here are three high-payoff things you can do that will bless the woman you love and keep you out of hot water.

1. Tell the truth. Didn't your momma always say to tell the truth? And keep in mind that she already knows the answer before she asks the question. She's asking for confirmation rather than information.
2. Confront her shame. Your words carry tremendous power, which is why you can't answer the question with just a yes or a no.
3. Confirm her loveliness. Remember the question really isn't just about the dress or her weight. There is something bigger at play.

But just in case you forget these three things, remember this: "We'll Leave the Light on for You!" at Motel 6.

2
"DO YOU NOTICE ANYTHING DIFFERENT ABOUT THE HOUSE?"

I (DAVID) WENT with a friend to hear some live music last night. You can hear great songwriters on any night of the week in Nashville, and when I was in my twenties, I went to hear live music all the time. Now that I am no longer in my twenties and I have a wife, three kids, two dogs, a mortgage, and a Volvo station wagon, I just don't get out on the town very often. If I do, I'm on my way to pick up soy milk at the grocery store, and I'm listening to the local alternative radio station on my way. So, needless to say, I was excited when my friend called to invite me, and my wife gave me the okay to revisit my youth.

Connie was engaged in some recipe research as I headed

for the door. She was sitting at our kitchen table, surrounded by cookbooks, making notes on a tablet. I kissed her forehead and bounded for the door.

It had been so long since I'd gone out that I couldn't really remember what you wear to go hear live music. I think it's like grungy jeans and a T-shirt with some kind of political or sarcastic remark on the front. So, I dug through my drawers and found a pair of jeans that were kind of faded, frayed, and had a big hole in the back pocket, but I wasn't sure if I could still button them. None of my T-shirts are very hip. I do have one from my favorite neighborhood coffee shop and one from Ben & Jerry's that says, "Save room for dessert." But I always feel self-conscious wearing it because the writing is really big on the front and it hugs my flabby stomach as if to say, "Yeah, baby, I *always* save room for dessert."

So, I gave up trying to dress like a twenty-year-old and just put on one of my plaid button-down shirts from J. Crew, like a good thirty-year-old man who has three kids and really isn't cool anymore. I put on my high-top Chuck Taylor's with this ensemble, and my wife, who had called a girlfriend for a consultation on cake batter consistency, started laughing hysterically when she saw me. She had to apologize to her friend while she gained composure. I heard her say something like, "I'm sorry, can you hold on a minute while I help my husband try to act his age?" So I took off the Chucks and put them back in the far corner of my closet floor.

When I arrived and paid the cover charge at the door, I asked the bouncer if he needed to see my ID before he stamped my hand. He looked at my graying hair, laughed, and said, "No, man, you look legal to me." I asked him if he was sure and he said, "Look, if you wanna show it to me, that's fine, man . . . whatever."

I walked into the smoky, dark, and loud club to find my friend. *This is awesome*, I thought to myself. *Just the way I remember it.* A lot of girls were looking at me, probably wondering if I was the artist's uncle, who'd come in from North Carolina to catch the show. I just smiled and moved through the crowd, like a proud uncle would. I got myself a drink, found my friend, and the opening act took the stage. They were loud—like, really loud—and I wondered if everyone else thought they were loud or if it was just me becoming like my parents when they'd say, "Turn that garbage down. You're going to ruin your hearing." (I didn't say a word for fear that it was the latter). I couldn't really understand what the lead singer was saying, but I acted like I could, nodded my head periodically, and enjoyed my beer. I called Connie so she could hear how loud the music was through the phone. She responded by saying, "That's great, sweetheart . . . you have a good time. I'll see you in the morning."

Once the screamers finished their set, this gal took the stage with her acoustic guitar and unassumingly started singing really deep, rich songs. About six songs into the set, she called up this guy who had a low, gravelly voice, and he sang a duet with her. He was so freakin' cool. He had grungy jeans on, and he could still button his. He had a bed-head thing going on with his hair . . . you know, like he just woke up with his hair looking all crazy and cool, and he meant for it to look like that. (When I wake up, my hair is always sweaty and greasy and mashed to my face on one side. I look more like a band kid with a learning disability that you just wanna help out). With eyes closed, he was turning his head from side to side to the beat of the percussion player and handling the microphone.

He sang lyrics that said something like, "So long, it's been so long, so long since I've held someone. Your headlights once would haunt my walls, but now they're miles away." *Who says that kind of stuff?* I thought to myself. *If I gave it my best effort, I couldn't be that cool.* But I gave it a good try in the bathroom mirror that night when I got home around 1:15 a.m. I'm a real rock star in the privacy of my home; you should see me work it.

The next morning, I woke to the sounds of my wife working in the kitchen. It was 7:00 a.m., and the kids were still asleep. When my kids are still asleep after 7:00 a.m., I always worry about things like carbon monoxide poisoning. I usually ask my wife if we should check their pulses or see if they're still breathing. I stumbled into the kitchen to find Connie making cupcakes for my twin sons to share with their little preschool classmates in celebration of their fourth birthday. Her research from the night before was strewn throughout the kitchen.

I watched her work, enjoyed the unusual quiet of sleeping children, and told her about my night on the town—how the bouncer wouldn't card me, how the guy with the gravelly voice nodded his head and handled the microphone, how I met Mindy Smith (one of the guest artists whose work I love) and didn't embarrass myself the way I usually do when I meet famous people.

Connie was sort of listening to my ranting, but sort of *not* listening. She was very distracted with her cupcakes. You see, my boys are allergic to all things dairy, so they have all these restrictions on what they can eat. My sweet wife works so hard to find recipes that can be altered so my boys don't miss out on the normal things kids love to eat like cookies and cupcakes. She does a great job substituting the milk and eggs in the recipes, but periodically it just doesn't turn out. Sometimes it takes real butter and whole milk to make a recipe work.

My wife is truly an artist. She has this extraordinary gift of creating beauty out of so many things. In addition to cooking, she loves to garden. There are flowers growing throughout our home and yard—in the beds in front of our house, behind our house, in pots on the porch, in the kitchen, everywhere. And there are fresh-cut flowers in antique jars and vases throughout our home, a testimony to her artistry.

She also grows fresh herbs, which she uses to create amazing dishes. She loves to linger in the kitchen, experimenting with recipes and foods. She has a particular passion for baking. (And if you look at my stomach, you get a real picture of this gifting). This is one of the many ways my wife loves and celebrates our children. Every year on their birthdays, she makes their favorite cake or cupcakes. She does it for me on our anniversary, Valentine's Day, and other special occasions. (She did draw the line with me when I asked for seven-layer caramel cake one year on Flag Day.)

On this Friday morning, she was determined to make these killer cupcakes for the boys and their class. The kitchen looked like a minefield as she carefully poured the batter into all the little cupcake holders and slid her masterpieces into the oven. About that time, we heard the sound of little feet on the hardwood floors upstairs. The kid invasion took place, and a typical Thomas morning began to unfold. I jumped into our ritual of feeding, dressing, and packing up kids for school. We call it feed and fly.

Midway through the ritual, I heard sounds of despair coming

from the kitchen. I made my way downstairs and there stood Connie, an oven mitt on her right hand, lamenting her sacred creation. The cupcakes were descending rather than ascending. They had all caved into a pool of oozy dough in the center. I didn't say a word. I just waited silently, watching my wife closely for a cue.

She moved frantically to the counter, where she had created homemade icing. Next to the icing was a stack of at least a dozen cookbooks. Connie had obviously spent over half the evening searching for cupcake and icing recipes that would be both dairy-free and delicious. There were notes all over the tablet about what could be substituted for various items.

She attempted to ice one of the doughy, volcanic-shaped cupcakes. She looked near tears as she spread the creamy substance and watched it ooze down into the volcano toward the bottom of the cupcake holder. It was getting worse by the minute.

She put down the knife and asked, "Do you notice anything about this cupcake?" She spoke again before I could answer. "What do you think when you look at this? Be honest with me."

Here's that moment, men. The loaded question has officially started ticking. The next words are critical—extremely critical. I didn't speak for a few seconds. Then I looked gently at her and said, "I love how much you love to do this and how, even if our kids don't fully appreciate it now, someday they will remember every time their mom labored for hours in the kitchen making something they love."

Touchdown! As the last word crossed my lips, I was thinking to myself, *You nailed it, buddy. That's as good an answer as any man could hope to give to that question.* But she came back to me wanting more.

"Thank you. Sometimes I do wonder if all this even matters to them. But I need you to tell me what you really think about these cupcakes."

There was no avoiding the question this time, although I tried. (It only made things worse.) "Well, you know for me it's not at all about how it looks, but how it tastes. I've told you before, honey, it all just ends up in the digestive system at some point." As the words crossed my lips, I thought to myself, *Man, you just swung from one end of the spectrum to the other. You went from affirming her artistry to basically saying who cares, because it's all coming out the colon eventually.*

Where did I go so wrong?

She looked deflated and came back with, "David, you know presentation matters to me when it comes to food. And look at these ridiculous cupcakes. I'm not sending these to school."

I tried to redeem myself. "Sweetheart, I'm sure it had every-thing to do with having to substitute. You yourself have said that removing or substituting core ingredients can affect the outcome greatly." As I was speaking, I could tell it meant absolutely noth-ing to her. So I made a last ditch effort. "Connie, these kids are four, they just want it to taste real sugary. Just pour a bunch of sprinkles in the middle and no one will ever notice . . . and those kids will love you."

The tears came streaming down her face as she grabbed for her purse. "I'm going to the store to buy some Rescue Hero popsicles." She raced for the front door as I looked helplessly at the kitchen, covered in sugar, flour, icing, and soy milk. I tried the iced cupcake. It was amazing. A little doughy, but amazing.

DEAD OR ALIVE

Most guys at this point scratch their heads and ask the question (either aloud or in their heads), What's the big deal?

Good question. What *is* the big deal? Why the tears? Whether it be cupcakes or curtains, when a woman creates beauty, she is functioning as she was designed. It's not so different from men and their performance at work. Consider the dude with the bed-head and the low, gravelly voice. That guy is making great art. It's his work, his passion. That guy is doing what he's designed to do. And you could tell it when he sang and commanded the stage.

I have a buddy named John who is a surgeon. He is a highly skilled physician who sees the work he does as art, because he is functioning according to his gifts and what he believes strongly is his calling. The guy can make a kidney transplant sound like an action flick. It has everything to do with his passion for medicine.

My wife is an educator by training. Her undergraduate work was in special education, and she has a master's degree in child and family studies. She has a particular passion for working with children with special needs. She has worked in hospitals, schools, and therapeutic homes, and she is so alive when interacting with kids with physical, emotional, and learning challenges.

In addition to nurturing children's lives, my wife is alive when she plants and nurtures things in her garden. When she arranges fresh-cut flowers throughout our home, it goes from being a ninety-year-old house with rickety uneven floors and windows that won't open, to this sanctuary of beauty and warmth. Her handprint is stamped throughout the place where we live. Her artistry is on display and it's stunning.

When my wife labors over recipes and creates amazing foods from a counter full of ingredients, she is living fully from her design. That moment when one of our kids looks to her with chocolate dripping from his little mouth and says, "Mommy, this is the best cookie I've ever had," she feels delight in his pleasure. She enjoys sharing what she has to offer with the people she loves.

HOME SWEET HOME

A guy walks in late from work and is enthusiastically greeted by his wife. She's beaming, smiling from ear to ear. It's obvious to the guy that she is excited about something more than seeing him. Curious, he asks, "What?"

"What, what?" she responds.

"What are you so excited about?"

"Can't you tell?"

Now, at this point the guy is thinking to himself, *If I could tell, why would I be asking?* But he's smart enough to not say that. So he just smiles and says something like, "No. What is it?"

"Notice anything different?" she flirtatiously inquires.

"Did you get your hair cut? Your hair looks great," he tries.

"No." She responds, looking confused. "It's not about me."

"Then what's it about?" he asks.

"About the house. Do you notice anything different about the house?"

He's bamboozled. "About the house?" He scans the room looking for anything that might be different or new. "About the house?" he asks again.

"Yeah. You don't notice?" She's now in disbelief at his obvious oblivion.

"New curtains?" he guesses.

"Nope." *Swing and a miss. Strike one!* Her smile is rapidly fading.

"A new lamp?"

"A new lamp?" she says begrudgingly. "I got that lamp months ago." *Strike two!*

Flustered and desperate he blurts out a response. "I don't know. What is it?" *Strike three. You're out!* He's blown it. She's angry and dejected. He's angry and guilty.

For some men, this simple question, Do you notice anything different about the house? can be as puzzling as Newtonian physics. It catches guys off guard—especially when they discern no obvious changes. These moments feel like an interrogation, only without the blinding lamp and the two guys playing good cop/bad cop.

Or like when a woman asks a man, "What color do you want to paint the bedroom?" and she holds out paint swatches. He sees various shades of brown, ranging from light brown to medium brown to dark brown. A woman, on the other hand, sees tan, coffee, chocolate, and russet. And *she* surely knows that he only sees brown. So why the heck is she asking it in the first place? What's behind the question, Do you notice anything different about the house?

Now, *that's* a good question. Men have the notion that women's questions are not always what they seem to be on the surface. Most guys have been burned in the past by these kinds of questions, so they're a little gun-shy about taking another bullet. Most women know that most guys don't have a clue about what's different, so they wonder if men even care. So what's with the question? Why is she trying to elicit his opinion?

Even though the woman may have a legitimate reason for asking the question, most of these loaded questions are often just clever ways to disguise statements. Women (and men, too, for that matter) often hide their true thoughts, wants, and feelings behind questions. They use questions as a way to avoid declaring their true feelings and making definitive statements.

You see, behind most questions, there's typically a statement. For example, when a woman asks, "Do you want to go with me and help me pick out new carpet?" she's more than likely saying, "I want you to do this with me."

Women are as creative as they are nurturing. For women who are typically caregivers, being creative outside of decorating the house can make them feel guilty. It's seen as impractical and selfish to take time out for themselves to create what is in their hearts. For many of these women, the home becomes a canvas for their expression. It is a way for them to simultaneously care for those they love and express their hearts. So, when a woman asks the question, Do you notice anything different about the house? what she is really asking is a question much closer to, Do you see my creativity, and does it move you?

My (Stephen's) wife, Heather, is a very creative woman with an affinity for revealing beauty. She is also rather eclectic. Her interest in art began early in our marriage and has taken her into exploring many different ways of expressing herself. In our little more than a decade of marriage, she has dabbled in a variety of art forms, including jewelry, sewing, mosaic tile, calligraphy, knitting, crochet, folk art/painted furniture, soap, cards/stationery, photography, stained glass, pottery, and various other endeavors that have involved miscellaneous art supplies from glue guns to floral tape to felt to fabric. Currently, Heather is taking violin lessons, and she is very interested in learning about woodworking. (I guess it's only a matter of time until she's wielding a jigsaw.)

To my dear wife's credit, she is very talented and enjoys learning new ways to express herself. (She's even made a good bit of money at a few of these endeavors.) On the downside, we have an attic full of art supplies spanning a number of mediums. It took me several years to learn to appreciate her shift from art form to art form. It wasn't until I learned to see how excited she became when she engaged her creativity that I really appreciated her for more of who she is—eclectic and all.

Recently, we had a birthday party with a tea party theme for our daughter, who turned six. Heather is masterful at hosting birthday parties for our kids. Typically, every element is tied to a theme and the theme is subtly repeated over and over until beauty resonates like a chorus. However, it can get a little intense with all the party planning. Leading up to the most recent party, I remember us having several conversations about which ribbon to use, which party favors would be best, cake vs. cupcakes, which dress our daughter would wear, round and round and round.

Whatever her quirkiness, Heather comes by it honestly. Her mother has a thirty-foot-long storage room full of all kinds of crafty tools and trinkets. She keeps every scrap of ribbon, every recycled gift bag, and anything else that she might imagine using someday—like the boxes that her checks come in, because there just might be a day when she will have a small gift to wrap. Once every couple of months, she spends a week organizing her collection, only to have it in disarray within a few days after exercising a creative frenzy.

I must admit that Heather's mom really does have a knack for cobbling together pieces of this and that to make something look beautiful. One clear mark of her creativity is redeeming beauty—finding something that has lost its shine and making it sparkle again. This creative ability to redeem beauty extends to her deepest, most secretive passion: the Goodwill store.

Her Goodwill obsession is more of an illness really, a disease, an addiction. There's a fine line between creative and kooky, and my mother-in-law straddles the line. She regularly drives two hours round-trip in her large SUV, spending who knows how much in gas, to rummage through the main Goodwill distribution center. It's there that she buys clothes by the pound—yes, by the pound (who knew?). She typically goes on Wednesdays, because on Wednesdays, clothes cost 99 cents a pound instead of the regular $1.49.

She typically buys bags and bags of clothes that she will generously give to her grandkids, sell at various consignment stores, or donate back to the Goodwill if all else fails. The other day, she was "shopping," if you can really call rummaging through mostly deceased people's garments shopping, when she found a shirt that she thought would look great on her husband. She examined it for wear and tear, and finding none, she proceeded to the checkout counter. She was in the checkout line before she realized that it was a shirt she had donated a few weeks earlier. She was buying her own shirt.

TWO OF A KIND

During the last century, the concept of women bearing a different nature than men took a beating. It was a fashionable trend in twentieth-century feminism that tried to dump the label *woman* because it was a flawed and oppressive term. Lately, more and more writers (psychologists, sociologists, theologians, etc.) are arguing for the need to reevaluate and examine the importance and uniqueness of the feminine. The Bible has always done this—starting with the first woman, Eve.

Names in Scripture, especially in the Old Testament, often tell us something significant about the person. The name *Eve*, which in Hebrew means "life-bearer," certainly explains something about the first woman; but because Eve is a female archetype, her name and nature also give us a clue into the biblical worldview of what is feminine. Women are uniquely designed to bring out beauty (whereas men tend more toward structure and order).

There are two creation stories in the Bible. The first (in Genesis 1:1-31 and 2:1-4) explains how the earth came into being and how God created everything in the universe. In this creation story, the universe progressively comes into being—moving from nothing to fullness. This story is action oriented. It's a masculine story.

The second story of creation (in Genesis 2:4-25 and 3:1-24) tells about God, Adam, and Eve in the Garden of Eden. This story illustrates the tension between good and evil. It explains how things were intended to be, and how division between Adam and Eve brought sin, shame, and suffering into the world. It has a more feminine accent. It is far more about relationship than structure.

In the second version of the story, God creates Adam but sees that something is wrong. "It is not good for the man to be alone," God says.[1] So God makes Eve and calls it good. Eve, being formed from Adam's rib, is of the same flesh and the same bone. What the Bible is getting at is that from the very beginning men and women cannot be complete without each other. Men's and women's lives intertwine so completely that neither can survive without the other—especially in the realm of creativity.

Adam and Eve are given a perfect world, but they are also given the ability to muck it all up. We all know the story. Confronted by the serpent, Eve makes a choice; she chooses the sweet fruit. She gives it to Adam. He doesn't say a word to stop any of this, and he eats the fruit. The result? Perfection is destroyed and true intimacy is lost.

These two creation stories suggest that in a perfect world, men and women are equal cocreators and costewards. Using Genesis 1, 2, and 3 as a lens, we see that men and women were made to cocreate. But how does all this help us better understand the question, Do you notice anything different about the house?

We often use words such as *he* and *his* to describe God, but strictly speaking this is incorrect, because God is neither male nor female. From the creation account in Genesis, he could be understood as encompassing both the male and female aspects. At creation's pinnacle, God conjured up beings "in his own image, . . . male and female he created them."[2]

What does "in his own image" mean? Like God, people have a nature that is fundamentally relational and creative. We are made to dream, create, imagine, and transform the world together. Adam and Eve were put in the garden to tend to it together. In the creation story, men and women were created for the same purpose but with slightly different expressions of God's image.

The question, Do you notice anything different about the house? and a man's subsequent cluelessness are direct echoes of what happened with the first man and woman.

A woman who asks this question is inviting a man to join her in the celebration of creating without exposing her heart to his participation or input. Eve did this in the Garden. She saw the snake and talked with it, but she didn't directly point it out to Adam. It's like she was waiting for him to say something first.

A more honest statement would be, "Hi, honey. I'm so glad you are home. Will you look at what I did today? I really want you to celebrate this with me, be curious about me, and tell me what you think about what I've done." A woman's question is a refusal to be vulnerable with her heart. It's a setup for the man to fail.

But don't think for one second that this takes the man off the hook. When a man fails to notice what is going on around him, he is just like Adam in the Garden—disregarding the snake and silently eating the fruit. The consequence of a man being oblivious is always chaos and shame and loneliness for his female counterpart. When a man fails to notice what is different about the house, it directly reflects his lack of attentiveness to his piece of paradise.

It's way more than cupcakes and curtains. It's artistry. And the question is so much deeper than if you noticed anything different about the house or what you thought of the cupcakes. The real question is, Am I creative? or Do you see beauty in my offering?

HERE'S THE POINT

"Do you notice anything different about the house?" is just the tip of the iceberg to a much bigger question. The real meat and potatoes question of a woman's heart is this: Do you notice my creativity, and does it move you? So, remember this, guys:

1. Pay attention. Keep your eye on the ball.
2. Encourage her creativity. Whenever your wife or girlfriend begins to move toward expressing herself, it is your opportunity to help remove whatever obstacles will impede her ability to express herself and God's creativity.
3. Delight in her offerings. Authentically celebrate whatever it is she creates. Be curious about it. Find out things like, How long did it take to complete? What was the process like? How much effort went into it? What does *she* like about it?

3
"DO YOU THINK THAT WOMAN IS PRETTY?"

MY (DAVID'S) PARENTS are musically inclined. They both sing (my dad, who has a degree in music, can actually sing extemporaneously in several languages), and they both play piano. Our home was always full of music—classical, R & B, rock, folk, instrumental—you name it, we heard it. I can remember being about seven or eight and dancing in the kitchen with my mom and sister to her old Paul Revere and the Raiders records. We heard everything from Luciano Pavarotti to Diana Ross and the Supremes, from the New York Philharmonic to the Beatles.

With my parents' giftings, you'd think I'd have the music gene. That would make sense, wouldn't it? Well, let's just say this: You know how two brown-eyed, olive-skinned brunettes sometimes give birth to fair-skinned, freckled redheads, and we all just scratch our noggins and wonder? That was the case in my household.

But my parents didn't give up without a good fight. I really can't carry a tune, but I can play an instrument or two. Well, kinda. When I was a kid, my folks required me to take piano lessons. They let me quit when I began slamming my forehead into the keys every time I was forced to practice. "It just wasn't worth the battle," my mother laments as she reflects on my "musical" days (she always looks like she needs a stiff drink when she talks about it). Following my stint with the piano, they recommended I try another instrument. They talked me into playing the trumpet in the sixth-grade band for a while. I wanted to be a drummer, though. Man, I wanted to be a drummer. A hair-slinging, sweat-dripping, women-screaming-my-name-at-the-stage, rock star kind of drummer. The band director told me that it didn't take nearly as much talent to play the drums as it did the trumpet, and that I showed way too much potential as a musician to play the drums. (Yeah, right, he just needed some warm bodies in the brass section.) What a lousy sales pitch! Middle school boys don't care about musical talent. I wanted to look cool and get the chicks, and everybody knows chicks don't dig guys who play the trumpet.

Well, I hung it up after a short exploration with the trumpet, the flügelhorn, and the French horn. I played the radio for the rest of my adolescence and then decided in my early twenties to try my hand at the guitar. I took some lessons for a few months with this hip musician in Nashville and bought a great acoustic guitar. I tried to learn some John Hiatt songs, and I would scream and yell like he does on "Slow Turning." I would thump the neck of the guitar and strum dramatically. I was pretty good as long as I stayed in my own head.

But one day, my guitar teacher gathered enough courage to gently say, "David, I wanna shoot you straight. I'm not convinced the guitar is your instrument. I don't know what your instrument might be, but I don't think it's this one. I think you might be wasting your money and my time." *Ouch!* So, I put my guitar in storage. I'm still confident I am destined to be a drummer. Someday I'll get around to getting me a set.

So, although I had no hopes of being a singer, I did get a gig in the music industry. It had nothing to do with my own musical pursuits (or lack thereof). I had just finished my undergrad and I had a BA in psychology. I knew I wanted to take some time off before I went to graduate school. The problem is that you're pretty limited in what you can do with a BA in psychology. You can be a manager at Baskin-Robbins, you can do landscaping, you can be a barista at Starbucks, or you can teach aerobics at the YMCA. (I had a friend from college who put her psych degree to use this way. According to my friend, there are a lot of whacked-out people who take step aerobics.)

I discovered that if you *do* want to work in the field, you have to take a case-management-level position, which is the mental health equivalent of being the fry guy at Mickey D's. I considered it a trade-off so that I could get some experience and decide if I even *wanted* to be a therapist. So, I applied and got hired at an inpatient facility that treats male adolescent sexual offenders. My third day on the job, a boy defecated and spelled his name on the wall with it: R-O-B smeared in human feces on the bathroom wall. I quit later that day and went to see what the pay would be for a position at Baskin-Robbins.

After a couple of days passed and I had a chance to recover from the poop incident, I gave working with kids a second chance. I applied to be a substitute teacher at a large public school. On my second day, an adolescent girl put her hand on my bottom in the hallway and made some racy, sexual remark to me. I was twenty-two at the time, but I looked not a day over eighteen. I couldn't tell if she thought I was a new student and just wanted to introduce herself to me (in a pretty aggressive kind of way), or if she knew that I was a substitute teacher and that was just her way of initiating the young male instructors. Either way, it kinda freaked me out. You see, where I attended high school in a little rural town, you just didn't touch your teachers on the bottom.

So, I thought about Ben & Jerry's. I liked that chain better anyhow, and I was sure they treated their employees well and paid more. Besides, I am more passionate about Chunky Monkey and Oatmeal Cookie Chunk than I am about most things in life. The hesitancy was that I knew they'd ask if I had any experience in the ice cream industry. And I did. I'd worked at Dairy Queen when I was fifteen. But I got fired for being too generous with the Blizzard toppings. Besides, what I really wanted to do was travel. If the plan was to enroll in grad school and commit two to four more years of my life to education, I wanted to spend some time seeing the world before I settled back in to academia.

Through a mutual friend, I met this amazing woman who had just signed a record deal. She was looking for a road manager when she traveled and a personal assistant when she was home writing and recording. I told her I'd never worked in the music industry and I didn't know what I was doing, but I had a psych degree, and I was sure that would count for something. She said it was okay, because she'd never made a record before and gone on tour. As long as I was flexible, could work crazy hours, and was open to being on the road, we'd both figure it out as we went along. Awesome!

It was an amazing gig. I went to New York, Seattle, Dallas, Portland, Canada, South America, all over the place. I'm a small-town boy, and I hadn't seen half the world. I loved every minute of it. It was the best excuse I had come up with not to go back to grad school. Nobody was defecating on the wall or touching my bottom, and I didn't have to serve ice cream to make ends meet. (I could just eat it, which is what I'd rather do anyway.)

The artist I worked for was married to a famous record producer. He produced big-name artists, and I got the chance to meet a lot of famous people during my tenure in the music industry. That was another perk to the already great gig I was enjoying.

One day while her husband was in town, he mentioned to me that he was working on a new project and that some well-known folks might be stopping by the home studio at different times. One of them was Dolly Parton. My boss and her husband warned me about how often people meet Dolly and completely humiliate themselves. I could understand why. She's this megastar. She's won every award known to man. She's one of the most famous artists in country music, a movie star. She's, you know, Dolly Parton. And in addition to her talents, there are her . . . assets. I won't say any more than that; we are all aware of her assets.

I was almost offended that they didn't know me well enough to know that I'm not the kinda guy who would be stupid enough to stare at her assets. Give me some credit. I do have a psych degree.

The possibility of a star encounter had honestly slipped my mind by the afternoon, because we got slammed with setting up some road dates and working with promoters. I remember being on the phone with a concert promoter in South Bend, Indiana, and having to pee in the worst way. I wrapped up the call and ran to the bathroom across the hall from my office. I was midway through relieving myself when I heard laughter coming from the hallway outside the bathroom. It was an unmistakable laugh. A high-pitched trademark laugh that anyone in the world would recognize as that of Dolly Parton.

Oh crap! Dolly Parton is freakin' standing in the hallway, a mere few feet from me. This megastar is outside the bathroom door. I finished up (which took even longer, because by now I was really nervous), washed my hands, checked myself in the mirror, wet down the part of my hair that was sticking up, dried off my hands, and opened the restroom door. There she was . . . Dolly Parton! She was so close to the door that I couldn't fully exit the bathroom.

"Well, howdy, you must be David. I've just been hearing about you," she said with her trademark smile. She had on a yellow sequined dress (a very fitted, short, low-cut dress) and yellow high heels. Her hair was platinum blonde and perfectly coifed.

"Yes, ma'am, I'm David. It is such an honor to meet you, Miss Parton," I said as my neck and face turned red. *Did I just say "ma'am" and call her "Miss Parton"? Am I six or twenty-two? David, what's wrong with you?* (At that point, I think I put my hands in my pockets after I shook hers and had this nervous little boy, aw-shucks thing going on with my posture.)

Fortunately, the grown-ups present picked up the stilted conversation and rescued me from the awkward pause. There we stood, just chatting it up. Me and Dolly. I kept saying to myself over and over in my mind, *Keep your eyes on her face. Keep your*

eyes on her face. Do not look at her very low-cut sequined dress.
Keep your gaze focused on her extremely large, unmistakable
eyes. Her eyes, her eyes, her eyes!

By this point in the exchange, it was no mystery to me why
I had received coaching regarding being in her presence. She was
mesmerizing: her beauty, her charisma, her voice, her presence.
She was just so Dolly Parton. She is one of the tiniest human beings I have ever met (okay, some parts are not very tiny). But she
is so petite, with a waist about the size of my wrist and flawless
skin. She was perfectly made up, like a Barbie doll.

She was every bit as funny in person as she was in interviews
or performances. And there we were just yakking it up like two
old friends catching up on years of missing out on each other's
lives (except I wasn't really talking). I was just kind of laughing—laughing and staring a lot.

We finished our conversation (the one where all I'd really
said was "yes, ma'am" and "Miss Parton") and she announced she
needed to get to the studio. She shook my hand again as she prepared to leave. As I dropped my hand back to my side, it brushed
across the tip of my shirttail. The part of my shirttail that I discovered was hanging out of the zipper of my pants and covering
half my boxers (my blue boxers with juggling monkeys on them).
The other half of my boxers was peeking out of my zipper.

She turned to walk down the hall (it was really a saunter
with some heavy sass and a pinch of prissiness in it) and I looked
down to see my pants wide open, exposing my shirttail (like a
hanky) and revealing the juggling monkeys. In all my excitement
to run out of the bathroom and meet Dolly Parton, I had forgotten
to "xyz." So I'd just had a whole conversation with Dolly Parton

with my fly open. My only prayer was that she never sees much of what goes on in life below her upper torso, that her assets somehow shadowed the juggling monkeys. My hope was that the only way I *really* humiliated myself was with my dumb looks and those few stupid words I spoke.

As I walked around the corner to tuck the juggling monkeys back in and breathe, the phone rang in my office. I raced over to grab it and found out it was Connie, whom I'd just started dating at the time.

"Connie, I can't believe you called. You will not believe who was just standing in my office," I said, with continued disbelief myself.

"Who?" she asked with great curiosity.

"Do you want to guess or should I just tell you?" I decided to turn the conversation into a game of sorts. Connie had grown accustomed to my encountering various entertainers in the music industry during my stint in the business, so she would periodically be invited into this game of "guess the celebrity."

"Honey, I don't know who, just tell me," she remarked, obviously wanting to move ahead in the conversation.

"Dolly Parton. Can you believe that?" I paused, waiting for her response.

"You're kidding me!" she exclaimed.

"I'm not kidding," I responded, and then continued with, "and I didn't stare at her, you know . . . assets. I was very conscious not to stare. I had a lot of prompting, and I assure you I did not stare at them."

Connie paused and then said, "Well, you certainly are talking a lot *about* her assets to have not taken notice of them." I was taken off guard by this response, and it took me a minute to recover.

"Well, I think any man, or any woman for that matter, would be equally distracted in her presence. I think it's just what happens when you encounter Dolly Parton," I quickly defended myself.

"That may be so, but you seem particularly enthralled by it all. Do you think she's pretty?" she asked.

"Well, yeah, I guess. I mean, in a Dolly Parton sort of way. Why are you asking me this?" I questioned with an air of defensiveness.

Connie said, "Well, honey, you're the one who couldn't stop talking about her 'assets.' I'm not the one who began this conversation."

The conversation continued to go south. I found myself wondering how in the world I had dug myself into a hole that deep. I tried to rewind the dialogue in my head. About midway, it occurred to me that I was doing the thing that kids do when they've broken a lamp or a window. They start talking about what they didn't do so much that it's obvious to everyone that they clearly did it. Why would I so strongly feel a need to defend my actions, to announce on multiple occasions that I clearly had *not* taken a look at the assets when I clearly *had?* For Pete's sake, you can't be in the same room with Dolly's assets and not notice. What drove Connie to ask the question in the first place?

PUTTING YOUR BEST FACE FORWARD

Do you think that woman is pretty? This question is strong enough in the heart of a woman to drive an entire industry. We live in a cosmetic culture—literally. Analysts at Goldman Sachs estimate that $24 billion is spent on skin care and $18 billion on makeup.[1]

Many women (and men too) are far more consistent with their skin care routines than they are with their prayer lives. Beauty consumes us. Our culture sets impossible standards on beauty. Graphics departments at fashion magazines spend hours "touching up" the cover models' photographs . . . Photoshopping away a few pounds here and erasing a few blemishes there.

It doesn't stop with looks; it goes as far as how we smell. In the past decade, Americans spent $15 billion annually on perfumes and $38 billion on hair-care products. These statistics are overwhelming in light of the reality that it would take only $6 billion, in addition to current expenditures, to offer basic education to all people in developing nations, and only $13 billion to provide basic nutrition and health needs universally in the developing world, a little more than we spend on lip gloss and Chanel No. 5.[2]

And that's just from the neck up. Let's focus for a moment on money spent below the neck. We've already shared with you the stats on weight loss in this country. In addition, women spend ridiculous amounts of money on fashion. According to the NPD Group, a consumer and retail information company, American women spend $101.6 billion on clothing in one year.[3]

The cosmetics and toiletry industry spends more money on advertising than airlines, telephone services, and the beer industry combined. They are ready and willing to help women determine that "they're worth it."[4]

HE NEVER HAS A SECOND CUP AT HOME

I (Stephen) began my caffeine addiction when I moved to Seattle for graduate school. Residing in the center of the coffee universe, it was hard not to become caffeine dependent. No wonder. With fewer than fifty clear days a year, Seattle is the poster city for Seasonal Affective Disorder (SAD). Birthplace of plaid-clad Pearl Jam, Seattle is the U.S. suicide capital according to urban legend. While the suicide statistics are untrue, a few months of constant, cold drizzle and no sunshine will drive anybody to drink. And in this city, coffee is the drink of choice.

Though I had consumed my fair share of coffee drinks before relocating to the Emerald City, nothing could have prepared me for the abundance of coffee houses in the Pacific Northwest. Every corner has at least two chain-oriented coffee shops (like Starbucks, Tully's, or Seattle's Best) and frequently a locally owned establishment as well. This is not to mention the coffee shacks that are stationed every quarter-mile or so. These drive-through structures are about the size of a couple of porta-johns and allow instant caffeine refueling.

Statistics show that Seattle is one of the most unchurched cities in America. Only about 2 to 5 percent of the inhabitants attend church regularly, which would suggest they're not very devout. After living there for a time, I strongly disagree. Seattle is a highly devout city—Seattleites just worship coffee instead of God.

It didn't take long, a few months maybe, until I was hooked and worshipped the caffeine god like everyone else. Over the next several months my daily caffeine intake gradually increased. By the time I left two years later, my drink of choice was a twelve-ounce quad (that means four shots of espresso) skim milk sugar-free hazelnut latte—essentially liquid methamphetamines with steamed milk.

One day was like most every other day: temps in the low 50s, overcast with a 200 percent chance of rain. I was holed up in a corner booth at a U-district coffee house, distracted by a couple at the table next to me. Over the top of my laptop, I could inconspicuously observe the entire conversation. I wouldn't go so far as to call it eavesdropping, because they were talking loudly enough for anyone nearby to hear every word clearly.

The woman looked to be about twenty-five. The guy was a few years older—thirty at the most. By the way they were comfortably touching across the table, I guessed that they were dating. They were both attractive and stylish, and they oozed a rebellious, unshowered vibe.

The crux of their conversation jumped back and forth between some foreign film and a new band (neither of which I had heard of). It seemed all rather pretentious, and I felt kind of like an extra in *Before Sunset*, the guy badly masquerading as Ethan Hawke with the girl doing a decent impression of Julie Delpy. They were center stage, and I'm pretty sure they knew it.

At one point, they were talking about the movie, *"Le Bla Bla Bla"* (excuse me . . . the *film*), when a female barista walked by their table on her way to the back room. Ethan shifted his gaze from his date to the passerby, and for an instant, his eyes became locked on the woman's backside. It's rather obvious that Julie noticed this indiscretion about the same time I did, because her hands recoiled from her beau like she'd been bitten. She leaned back in her chair and crossed her legs, glaring at him over the top of her retro-styled glasses like only a woman scorned can glare—eyes smoldering with condemnation, resentment, and self-righteousness.

Realizing that he'd been far less subtle than he first thought, Ethan said what many a stupid man has said when caught in this same position, "What?"

Julie didn't flinch. Her only reaction to his impertinence was an ever-so-slight contraction of her brow so that her face had the beginning hints of a scowl. Incredulously Ethan called her bluff, badly feigning innocence. "What?" he said again. There was a slight pause in the conversation, just long enough for Julie to make sure she had his full and undivided attention.

"Do you think that woman is pretty?"

"Who?"

"Who? The woman you were just staring at."

"I wasn't staring at anyone." *I've gotta give it to this guy; he stuck to his guns.*

"No, you're right. You were staring at her butt!"

About this time, the barista in question came out from the back room, passing right back by the table. Julie reached out and gently grabbed the woman's arm, stopping her cold in her tracks. "Excuse me," she said with all the pleasantness she could muster. *Oh, this is getting good.*

"Yes. Can I help you?" the barista asked politely.

"No, but you might be able to help *him.* My boyfriend here was just admiring your tush. I thought he might want to meet you."

Ethan sank low in his chair—his urban coolness melting and quickly evaporating—while the two women scowled derisively at him. He looked more like a schoolboy busted by the teacher than the hipster he had been a moment earlier. I felt bad for my brother—not bad enough to say anything—but bad enough to look away, put in my earphones, and try to ignore the remainder of the conversation. Thankfully, within a few moments the couple got up and left. Who would want to witness a public castration anyway?

WHAT YA LOOKIN' AT, FELLA?

You may be aware of the Web site Hot or Not (www.hotornot.com). Launched in 2000, it has been featured in several Web sites, magazines, and newspapers, and it has even made *Entertainment Weekly*'s "It" List. In essence, the site is a place where people can post a picture of themselves and have other people vote on whether or not they are "hot." According to the founders of the Web site, more than 12 billion votes have been cast since its inception (and along with each vote has come the eradication of the concept of "inner beauty"). Am I beautiful? Do you think I'm pretty? or cute? or gorgeous? or ugly? Regardless of who asks the question and how it is asked, behind it is a much deeper question.

GLIMPSING GOD

"Do you think that woman is pretty?" What would drive any woman to ask this question? First of all, let's be honest; men don't really get asked that question unless they have a wandering eye or the woman asking is insecure. Second, the real questions being asked are, Do you see *me*? Do you see beauty in *me*? Do you see beauty in *me* the way you obviously see beauty in that other woman? Am *I* worth another glance?

This question, Do you see me? probably more than any question, is a question of the heart. Do you see me? is really a question that asks, Do I have significance to you? Do I matter?

Does the presence of my face bring you joy? Do you see me for who I am, and does that intrigue you? Do I capture your gaze and along with it your heart?

We are created as relational beings. We understand ourselves based on internal reactions (what we feel and think) to external people and things. Philosopher Martin Buber *(now that's an unfortunate name, isn't it?)* called this the "I/Thou" relationship. Buber argued that human existence may be defined by the way in which we engage in dialogue with each other, with the world, and with God. Simply meaning, we only know ourselves in relationship with others (the most *other* being God).

In the book of Genesis, we see that Adam had this kind of moment—a moment of knowing himself by encountering another being. Before Eve came on the scene, Adam filled his time farming, landscaping, and naming animals. He was lonely and lost. It wasn't good. He didn't really get a sense of himself. Then Eve showed up. When God placed Eve in Eden, Adam broke into poetry. He was moved internally, and he understood more fully who he was.[5] Eve, too, knew herself in reference to Adam, and both knew themselves in reference to God. This is what is meant by being created in God's image. It is a reference to who we are like, and it's how we most understand ourselves. Do you think that woman is pretty? and its underlying question, Do you see me? are attempts for women to find greater self-understanding and contentment. In this way, men have great power as God's image bearers to either bless or curse women. Through the eyes of noble and wise men, women can deeply experience the honor and glory of being a woman.

THROW ME A LINE

Do you think that woman is pretty? There's a lot at stake when the question is posed. A woman is wondering, *Do you see me just for my looks, or is there something more? Do I hold your gaze? Is there enough there to keep you interested?* In that moment, a woman is vulnerable to being forgotten. There is so much risk involved here: the risk of asking the question, the risk of hearing your answer. She is not only fearful of being compared, but she is fearful of being *abandoned*. Now, that word may sound strong, but the fear runs that deep. To lose your gaze to another woman is to abandon her beauty and her heart for some matter of time. She feels compared. She feels inadequate. She feels as if she has little to offer. That's what's at stake.

So, what's a guy to do? Let's take another look at my (David's) options with Connie in the midst of the Dolly dilemma. The options carry opportunity for speaking to a woman's longing as well as exposing a man's courage (or lack thereof).

Question: "Do you think she's pretty?"

- Option 1: "Honey, she's Dolly Parton."
- Option 2: "I didn't really notice."
- Option 3: "Nothing to write home about."
- Option 4: "Honey, she's a beautiful woman, not a woman I'm interested in being in a relationship with, though. A little top-heavy for my liking."

Option 1 is better known as a diversion. And women almost always recognize a diversion, regardless of how cleverly disguised it may be. The result is that she'll find her way back to the original question, and you won't be off the hook. Bottom line: A diversion is just a creative way of stalling and avoiding the inevitable. It also does nothing to address a woman's heart.

Option 2 is what we in the counseling field refer to as avoidance. It's really another form of stalling, only on a bigger scale. Women almost always recognize avoidance, although sometimes not for a while. Avoidance may get you off the hook for a longer period of time, but in the end, it may cause greater damage, because it typically involves some form of lying.

Option 3. Ahh, Option 3. Let's call this option playing it safe. Playing it safe is, in essence, another form of creative lying. I see an attractive woman; I try to pretend she isn't attractive when she is obviously incredibly attractive. I play down her beauty in an attempt to validate a woman I love and end up countering the effect. Bottom line: A woman can smell this a mile away. Just acknowledge the assets, and then let it be followed by truth spoken about the woman you are addressing.

Option 4. Didn't your mama always teach you to tell the truth? Don't you remember as a kid when your parent would say, "If you just tell the truth, you won't be in nearly as much trouble as if you aren't honest"? Same truth applies in this situation. Just tell the truth. Repeat that aloud at this moment. *Just tell the truth!* Tell the truth about the woman in question. Speak the truth about the woman asking the question. Name what you love about her. Name where you see beauty in her. Identify what you believe her question to really be about and what you long for her to know. And you can also handle it with some humor: "A little top-heavy for my liking." Humor can be a great way to break the intensity as long as it isn't used as a diversion or avoidance. It must be partnered with telling the truth.

HERE'S THE POINT

Don't forget guys, the real question is not, Do you think that woman is pretty? The real question is, Do you see me? Do you see beauty in me? Your job is to

- steer clear of diversion, avoidance, and playing it safe.
- tell the truth. If you were looking, admit you were looking. Tell the truth about the woman in question and then speak truth about the woman asking the question.
- name her beauty. Call out what you see in her character. Identify where you see evidence of her beauty and creativity.

And last, if you ever meet Dolly Parton, stay very focused on her eyes.

4
"WHAT ARE YOU THINKING ABOUT?"

WHAT **ARE YOU** thinking about? What *are* you thinking about? What
are *you* thinking about? What are you *thinking* about? What are
you thinking *about*?

No matter how you ask it, this modest little inquiry has the
potential to wreak havoc. This question may sound innocent, but
when in the wrong hands, it can be used to bring down the free
world. . . . Well, maybe it's not that big of a deal, but What are you
thinking about? has been relational dynamite for many a couple.

Almost every man and woman has a negative memory centered on this question. For a guy, it can seemingly come out of
nowhere, like a relational blitz. And once he is flushed from the
pocket, his only option is to mentally scramble like Steve McNair
on a cold November day looking for a way to turn near catastrophe

into a touchdown. For a woman, the question usually is an attempt to be more connected and secure in a relationship with a creature (a man) who is far less verbal, far less relationally oriented, and far more pragmatic. Perhaps more than any other loaded question, What are you thinking about? exposes the core insecurity of women and the foundational incompetence of men.

CZECH MATE

Picture this scene for a moment—two young twentysomethings, twenty-four hours into marriage. My wife and I (David) are in a red convertible, on a picturesque summer day, traveling down the open highway, fueled by young, innocent, naive love. My bride is next to me, her long blonde hair blowing gently in the wind. She has that glow about her that newlyweds have on their first day of marriage (following their first night of marriage).

Connie looks over at me and asks, "What are you thinking about?" (This is one of those moments when a wise man would say something like, "How thankful I am to spend the rest of my life with you.") Sometimes I'm that wise man, sometimes I'm not. On this particular day, I smiled as I looked back at her and responded, "I'm thinking about our future together. Let's make a list of everything we want to do in our life together before we have children. Let's each make a list in our heads and then write them all down." Now that's not such a bad response (especially for a newlywed), but hold on for where it goes from here.

She obliged me and pulled a pen and some paper out of her purse. After a little thought, I began rattling off things like raft the great rivers of the West, hike the Appalachian Trail, sleep outdoors somewhere in the Grand Canyon, get scuba certified in the Caribbean, buy a tandem bike, deep-sea fish in the Bahamas, purchase a canoe, and backpack across Europe. I decided to stop there; in my mind, that was a good starting point. I decided not to mention my idea of living in Costa Rica for six months, cross-country skiing in Canada, and a summer biking trip across New England.

Connie seemed paralyzed and had a look of subtle panic on her face. She very gently said, "Wow. Not one of those things made my list. I'm not quite sure what to do with that."

I immediately responded with, "That's okay. Just tell me what's on your list." She hesitated for a moment and then reluctantly began sharing her ideas. My wife's list included things like read Jane Austen aloud to each other, eat Chinese food every Christmas Eve, go see Shakespeare in the park in August, have breakfast in bed every anniversary while we watch our wedding video, pick fresh blueberries together in the summer and apples in the fall, and visit the local flea market once a month.

When she finished, we both sat in silence for a moment. It would be the first of a thousand moments in our marriage when one (or both) of us would think, *You're not quite the person I thought I married.* In the very first hours of our marriage, our differences were beginning to unfold.

Our lists are so reflective of our differences. I want to raft the great rivers of the West and backpack across Europe. My sweet bride wants to read Jane Austen aloud together in bed at night and pick fruit. I crave adventure, and my wife craves intimacy. It makes for some fascinating exchanges under our roof. Some days our marriage would make great material for a sitcom.

Well, life just happened, as it always does. Three months into our marriage, I decided to go back to graduate school, and we bought our first house, got a second dog, and began settling into life together. For the longest time I knew exactly where the honeymoon list was, and I'd pull it out from time to time.

We did manage to accomplish things on our honeymoon list. We found a B & B that we fell in love with, we read aloud to each other, we had breakfast in bed on a number of occasions, we took a few trips, we watched our wedding video every anniversary, we hiked with the dogs, and although we didn't buy a canoe, we rented a few. We hadn't made it to Europe, though. It just never seemed to be the right time. We couldn't afford it while I was in grad school, and once I graduated, we needed to pay off my school loans, and I needed to start a practice. My wife had been to Europe twice before—once in high school and once in college—so the desire to go didn't burn in her the way it did in me, having never been there before. Periodically, I would bring it up and she (being wise, practical, and financially responsible) would list all the reasons why we couldn't or shouldn't go.

At some point, (I don't remember exactly when) we began talking about starting a family. Actually, my wife did most of the talking in that conversation. I contributed only three words to the dialogue. I would simply say, "I'm not ready" every time she paused to take a breath. The conversation became more and more frequent, until she wouldn't accept "I'm not ready" as an answer anymore. I met with a friend and told him that Connie was no longer content with just me and two dogs and that I was wondering if getting another puppy would make a difference. He said I could get a whole litter of puppies and it likely wouldn't do the trick. I asked him if he was absolutely certain about the puppies, and he said he was.

With that dead end, I tried to squeeze Europe into the equation. "How about we go to Paris and make a baby?" It almost worked but not really. Next thing I know, we're pregnant. We didn't even get to try for very long, which is the only really good part about getting pregnant when you're not really ready to have a baby. No Europe, and no months of having great sex, trying to make a baby.

I remember thinking to myself, *Now we'll never get to Europe. If we couldn't afford it before, we certainly won't be able to now.* A couple of years passed, and my daughter had her first birthday. Then one night we were having dinner with our best friends, John and Kendra. Midway through the meal, John threw this question out on the table: "What would you guys think about going to Europe with us?" It turns out they were thinking about getting pregnant at some point in the near future and wanted to squeeze in some great travel before the plane was grounded. John, who had lived in Eastern Europe for part of his twenties and speaks Czech, knows his way around much of Europe, so he could act as our tour guide. This was a dream scenario in my mind. I looked at Connie and said, "Honey, this is it. Here's our opportunity."

She looked at me as if I had just suggested we do something ridiculous like go to Europe. She spoke in a whisper (the way you do to a friend when he doesn't know his fly is undone or he has a booger hanging out of his nose) and said, "Sweetheart, what are you thinking?" (There's that question *again*!) "Did you forget we have a one-year-old?"

I responded with, "Of course, I didn't forget we have a kid!" (Although looking back, I think I did forget for a minute because I was so excited by the idea of getting to Europe after waiting thirty years). Connie told John and Kendra we were honored they'd asked us and would consider their offer. (I whispered to them on the way out the door to go ahead and check on flights.)

After weeks of my begging and pleading, my wife *finally* gave in. Months later, we dropped off our daughter with my parents, and we hopped a plane to Munich. We started off in Germany, heading toward Austria. At the third country into the trip, my wife started getting a little teary. Actually, she was more than a little teary; she cried on and off all day because she missed our daughter. I was actually pretty sympathetic the first couple of days. It was our *first* child, and she had never been away from her for any period of time, much less for weeks across the globe from her. But the more my wife longed to be home and pooh-poohed my trip, the angrier I got.

John had arranged for the four of us to visit a spa town in the Czech Republic. I was certain a trip to the spa would jolt her out of her sadness (and me out of my frustration). What woman doesn't love a little pampering? So, we arrived in Marianske Lazne, a beautiful old Eastern European city.

When I think of a spa, I envision a bunch of rich women getting their eyebrows waxed, Swedish massages, manicures, seaweed facials, and foofy food that costs a boatload of money but tastes disgusting. But the Czech people define "spa" differently. Their spa services are fashioned out of a more medicinal approach, with a menu that might include anything from a colon cleansing treatment to a saltwater enema to a mineral bath. And if you do get a massage, it will likely be from a large woman named Hishta, who looks more like a WWF wrestler with hairy pits and legs than a masseuse—there is no light touch involved.

The first day in town, Connie and Kendra found a studio that offered manicures and pedicures on the south side of the city. Connie seemed to be in slightly better spirits, which freed me up to really enjoy myself. When John and I went for our massages, we were ushered into a marble room with steam and all these stones. It was like an ancient Roman men's locker room. We were handed a sheet and instructed to take our clothes off and enter the massage room. We noticed the other men draping their sheets like togas, so we attempted to do the same in keeping with the culture. I'd only worn a toga on one other occasion . . . at a fraternity party in college. I couldn't exactly remember how to tie it, so I just wrapped it around my body and held it tightly closed. We exited the locker room and entered an underground sanctuary with large columns and a marble pool. It all looked like something out of an ancient history textbook. That is, until we saw what occupied the pool—twenty saggy, elderly men swimming around *in the nude*.

Around the outside of the pool were some rooms with tables and large women in surgical scrubs performing massages on these old guys. Before your mind goes wandering off too far, they *were* legit massages. Nothing illegal or pornographic was taking place; it was just incredibly bizarre. Imagine a senior citizens' center swimming pool in the day of Helen of Troy and all the old boys swimming naked and then hopping out of the pool and getting rubbed down from Ms. WWF.

I looked at John and whispered, "I don't have issues with nudity, but I've just never been swimming with a bunch of naked old men." He laughed and said, "David, I tried to tell you it would be different. European people have different ideas about nudity and the human body." He went on to say, "If you don't want to get in the pool, just sit here and I'm sure they'll just usher you into the massage." So I did.

Every minute or so, a large woman would peek out to check on me, give me a strange look, and then disappear behind the curtain again. I smiled, waved, and kept looking at her with this look that said, *I'm ready now; I'm not going swimming with the cast from* Cocoon. *Can we please just get on with the massage?*

Eventually she came out and began giving me instructions—forceful instructions (in Czech)—while pointing at the pool. John, who was following protocol, was on the far side of the pool and couldn't hear what she said before she stormed off. He swam to the side of the pool, laughing at the sight of me in my toga getting wrung out in Czech by a large European masseuse. One of the old guys told John that she was attempting to tell me that I wouldn't fully benefit from the experience until I elevated my body temperature in the heated pool. This step is referred to as hydrotherapy and is considered to be a vital ingredient in the massage experience.

I realized, if this was the case, that she would never come for me unless I stripped down and swam around with the seniors. So I dropped my toga and did a quick cannonball into the pool.

Five minutes later, she did come for me again, but she just stood there. I said (in very clear English), "Hishta, I am not getting out of this pool until you close your eyes or go back in that room. Now hand me my toga and turn the other direction." She just stood there staring at me. We simply had not gotten off to a good start.

When I realized she wasn't budging, and I would never see her again anyway, I got out of the pool and streaked across to my toga.

Once we reached the table, Hishta and I began a friendly game of charades. She acted out how I should take off my toga, drape it on the massage table, and lie face down. I acted out asking, "Where's the towel to cover my behind?" She answered with the universal sign for "Say what?" Then it hit me. If the pre-massage involved swimming naked, what possibly made me think I would have a towel to cover my bum? So, once again I dropped my toga, she draped the massage table with it, and I jumped on. It was more like a doctor's table. You know, the metal kind with a strip of white paper down the middle. I endured being slammed, yanked, and pounded around for forty-five minutes like a piece of chuck roast being packaged by a butcher. I thought about my teary wife and prayed she was having a better time than this.

I couldn't wait to cover myself with my toga, go back to the locker room, and ask John if his massage had been as miserable and violating as mine. I later found out that he knew how to request, in Czech, that he preferred to be draped with a towel and use light to medium touch, and his masseuse accommodated him. I tried to just be thankful that Hishta hadn't accidentally done a colon check while I was on the table.

We joined our wives later that afternoon. *Their* experience had been wonderful—no nudity, no swimming with the elderly, nothing violent. They laughed hysterically as we told the story of our massage. Connie was smiling for the first time in twenty-four hours and I was relieved. We walked to the Colonnade in the center of the town before having dinner and returning to our hotel for the evening.

We had been in bed for about half an hour when Connie rolled over toward me and asked, "What are you thinking about?"

Here is that question again. *What would the wise man say in this moment?* Something like, "How thankful I am to be lying next to you in a foreign country. How much I miss our little girl and how I'm sorry you have felt so sad. But thank you for making the sacrifice to be here with me." Instead, I responded with, "I'm thinking about redeeming my spa day tomorrow. I think I'll have a mineral bath in the King's Suite. And I'm thinking about hiking in the countryside of Nove Mesto and hearing the symphony in Prague tomorrow night. And we haven't even gotten to Austria yet. We have so much more to see and do!"

All of a sudden, the question and the moment felt dangerously familiar—my long list of dreams, my passion for travel and adventure, the Bohemian lifestyle I could so easily live . . . and the differences. I looked over at my wife. Tears were beginning to stream down her face. She looked devastated and hopeless. "You love all this so much, don't you? You are lying here in bed, dreaming of all the places we have yet to see, and I am aching to be home. I miss our daughter so much that I can barely breathe. I can't sleep. I can't stop thinking about her. It is killing me to be here, and you can't take it in fast enough."

I lay there next to her, frozen and numb. It was one of many moments in our marriage when I was paralyzed by our differences. We are two incredibly different people, making this crazy, wonderful, complicated, beautiful, challenging attempt at sharing life together. It showed up in the first twenty-four hours of our marriage as I dreamed of rafting the great rivers of the West and she dreamed of breakfast in bed together at home. And now, here we were together in bed on the other side of the world—I was still dreaming . . . and she was weeping.

FOR EVERY QUESTION . . .

The question, What are you thinking about? is problematic on a number of fronts. First, this question is usually rather unexpected by the man. It most frequently comes right out of the blue, like when he's watching a game on television or he's quietly riding home at the end of a perfect date.

Though it may be well intentioned, this question throws a guy off balance. It forces him to analyze and assess what he is feeling, thinking, and experiencing and then put all that jumbled ethereal material into lucid sentences that clearly express all this. If you're a woman, you're probably thinking, *What's the big deal?* If you are a guy reading this, it's probably closer to, *You've got to be kidding me.* As action-oriented creatures with vastly different brain structures from women, men find that being at once intro-spective, collective, and articulate can be rather difficult. That's why so often men respond with simple grunt-like responses such as "Nothing" or "I dunno."

A significant problem with the question, What are you think-ing about? is that it comes loaded with assumptions. One assump-tion is that men are actually thinking something (which may not be true). A further assumption is that men want and/or need to talk about what they're thinking. Another problem with this question is that women assume that men think like women. When a woman asks a man this question, she can't always be sure she is going to get a satisfying answer. But if a man asks a woman this question, he will almost always get a thorough answer. I (Stephen) tested this theory on my wife the other day just to see what she would say.

It was late one weekend morning, and she had just come in

from the supermarket when I asked her what she was thinking about. Here's her response (off the top of her head, I might add).

"Right now, I'm thinking about putting away the groceries. I'm also considering what we're going to feed the kids for a snack. In addition, I'm thinking that I've been so busy this morning that I haven't eaten anything myself, and I'm really hungry now, so I'm trying to figure out when I can stop for a minute and eat. Beyond that I'm asking myself, 'When did I become the mother of four?' Our life is moving so quickly and changing so much. Where has all the time gone? Everything used to be so simple. Why did you ask? What are you thinking about, Stephen?"

"Who, me? Nothing. I was just curious."

Wow! Not only was she thinking about something, she was simultaneously thinking about four semi-connected things on four different levels: practically (groceries), logistically (when to feed whom), relationally (her relationship to our kids and me), and philosophically (her place in the world). Talk about multitasking. Men, on the other hand, are singularly minded. Usually, we *are* thinking, but since we don't think like women, we are usually thinking only about one thing. And that one thing can change at any moment without notice or obvious logic. So what are men thinking about? Here's a brief list:

- Food
- Work
- Sex
- Food
- Work
- Money

- Sports (baseball, football, golf, basketball, or whatever sport we are interested in)
- Food
- Sex
- Work
- God
- Sleep
- Food
- Sex
- Work
- Vacation
- Food

Though these topics are fairly consistent, there are always the random thoughts:

- If I could travel back in time, where would I go?
- What would I do if I won the lottery?
- Who would win in a no-holds-barred celebrity death match: Madonna or Britney Spears; Mike Tyson or Tonya Harding; Richard Simmons or Mr. Rogers?
- Who's cooler, Captain Kirk or Han Solo?

Sound weird? Not if you're a guy.

Obviously, we're being extremely stereotypical and a little sarcastic to help make a point: Men *are* thinking—it's just not how women are thinking. Though oversimplified, it's clearer to explain it this way: Men are only thinking about one thing at a time while women are thinking about everything else.

More and more, science is proving that women's and men's brains function in very different ways. Due to differences in body size, women typically have smaller brains than men, but both sexes have about equal average IQ scores. How come? Men have about 15 to 20 percent less gray matter than women. Gray matter is where the brain links thoughts, concepts, and associations. Women's brains are hardwired to think about more than one thing at a time—which explains why women tend to be great multitaskers. Guys' brains, on the other hand, are filled with more white matter. White matter helps with special reasoning and also allows single-mindedness and focus.

So you can see how the question, What are you thinking? exposes the male physiological deficiency at processing different types of information quickly and accurately. It's not that men are not emotional or relational. It's that men are not wired to process this kind of data the way women are.

Another problem with this question is that it is so straight-forward. Though men usually prefer things clear-cut and uncomplicated, the conclusiveness of this question is intimidating. With so little wiggle room, there is little that can be done to dodge it. Because of their perceived biological deficiency in this area, men can feel incompetent and trapped.

Additionally, this question is open-ended. Unlike yes or no questions, this question leaves plenty of rope to hang ourselves. Men know that there is no *right* answer, but we are all aware of the multitude of wrong answers. It's like a pop quiz that counts for 50 percent of the semester grade—and on top of it all, it's an essay test, not multiple choice, not true-false, not even fill in the blank. He knows that he won't be able to give an answer that will quickly and clearly express all that is going on in his head and heart. He also knows from experience that his vagueness can cause lots of problems in the relationship. If he sounds uncommitted in his answer, it probably has more to do with the fact that he is unsure of his inner world than it does with the fact that he is unsure of the relationship.

WHAT NOT TO SAY

There are several bad responses to this question, but perhaps the worst response came from television's Al Bundy *(Married with Children)*. When faced with this question by his wife, Peg, he answered, "If I wanted you to know what I was thinking, I would be talking to you." Ouch! For men and women to enter into this question together, they both need to know what is being played out.

Here is a *hypothetical* example. Suppose I (Stephen) am *hypothetically* driving in the car with my wife and there is *hypothetically* a momentary lull in the conversation. Heather glances over at me and asks, "What are you thinking about?" Now because this is *hypothetical*, we could be newly dating or married for fifty years or it could be our fifth wedding anniversary and we are on our way home from dinner. It doesn't really matter because it's *hypothetical*.

"Really?" I ask. "What am I thinking about right now?"

"Yeah. What are you thinking about?"

Now my being the guy that I am, I answer honestly, "I am thinking about something that happened at work yesterday." And before the sentence fully leaves my mouth, I can see disappointment on Heather's face. So I quickly try and add on to the end of the sentence, ". . . and I was thinking about you." *Hypothetical* or not, the moment is shot and I *hypothetically* will spend the rest of the ride home trying to repair and redeem the moment.

Relationally, what's at the core of this dynamic? Lurking behind the question, What are you thinking about? is a deeper, richer question, a much more honest and vulnerable question, something closer to, Are you thinking about us? For the woman, this question exposes her core insecurity—loneliness.

At the heart of every woman is a desire to be safe and connected. The most insecure feeling a woman can have is when she exposes her vulnerability, desire, and need for intimacy only to find that she's alone. Asking the question, What are you thinking about? is a way for a woman to protect herself from the possibility of rejection and isolation. Female security most often comes in the form of relationship.

It's so important to pay attention to what's at stake here. The tension that exists is one of God's great opportunities, an opportunity that is the bedrock for much growth and transformation in life, but one that may also drive us to the edge of insanity in some moments.

When my (Stephen's) wife asks the question, What are you thinking about? she is like many other women who are in relationship with men. She is hoping, desperately hoping, that I am thinking about *us*. Her hope is that my thoughts are turned toward our relationship—the way hers so often are. It takes little to no effort to turn her attention and focus to the state of our family. It comes so naturally that it's like breathing for her. In fact, it comes to her so easily that she has a hard time making herself *stop* thinking about the relationships that are important to her. Her thoughts are continually turned toward heart and home.

Does this mean women don't crave adventure or long for things other than relationship and romance and family? Absolutely not. Heather, for example, has a master's degree from one of the best universities in the country, and she is passionate about a number of different things like music, reading, or creating art. However, none of these things holds a candle to how passionate she is about our family. Nothing takes her to a place of more joy or more pain. And it threatens her relational security when she asks that question and finds that my mind is somewhere else.

IT'S ALL GOD'S DOING

In terms of relationship, the greatest pain in a woman's heart is loneliness. That's what is at the core of this question. When my mind and heart are somewhere else, it exposes Heather's desire for intimacy and how little control she has over sustaining it. Because we are so different, she can never do enough to hold my entire attention (outside of manipulation, deception, or threat). And when my attention is turned somewhere else, her greatest fears are realized.

For men, this is quite different. The same way women struggle with being lonely, men struggle with being effective and influential. We want our words and actions to have weight, longevity, and impact. The greatest threats to masculinity are futility and impotency—that whatever we say or do will lack power and will not last.

Men and women do relationships differently. Men find relational fulfillment in things like work, sports, or projects. They are collaborative (relational toward an outcome or a goal). Women, on the other hand, prefer communication, process, and connection (relationship *is* the goal). Men like to move into a challenge, keep score, win, and overcome, whereas women are more orientated towards relationships and nurturing.

Scripture speaks to this dynamic of loneliness and ineffectiveness in Genesis 3, the story of the Fall. As a result of Adam and Eve's disobedience, God doles out a series of curses. What's important to note is that these curses are given along gender lines.

A central part of the curse for women is relational inequity. According to Scripture, one of the consequences for Eve's disobedience to God is that she and Adam will no longer relate on a par with one another. To Eve God says, "Your desire will be for your husband, and he will rule over you."[1]

In the verse above, the man emerges as authoritative over Eve, whereas earlier in the story Adam and Eve were more collaborative. The result is that a man seeks to rule over a woman, and a woman schemes to take over a man's God-given authority. Collaboration and dependency are traded in for power and insecurity.[2]

With Adam, God is even more hard-hitting. He says, "Cursed is the ground because of you; through painful toil you will eat of it all the days of your life. It will produce thorns and thistles for you, and you will eat the plants of the field. By the sweat of your brow you will eat your food until you return to the ground, since from it you were taken; for dust you are and to dust you will return."[3]

Adam is representative of every male. Everything he endeavors to do will be hard work and will ultimately fall apart. He will have his heart bent toward accomplishment, but he will always fail in the end. Success is always fleeting. In short, the Curse does this: A woman will want to be in charge, but she can't be.

The man will have more power, but everything he is responsible for will fall apart.

The consequence for women: loneliness. The consequence for men: futility. No wonder having the fulfilling and intimate relationships we were created for is not only hard for men and women but is impossible.

There is beauty in all of this tension. What God does in the Fall is create a way that we will never ever be happy again apart from him. He creates a dynamic that says, "Though you were made for each other, you can never fulfill each other." You can't create your own fulfillment. Romance won't do it. Work won't do it. Kids won't do it. Money won't do it. Any life apart from God will ultimately be lonely and ineffective.

The curses for Adam and Eve become opportunities for dependence on God, obedience to God, and intimacy with God (all the things they shunned by listening to the serpent). That is the blessing. All of the relational difficulty between men and women is in the end meant to drive us crazy and drive us back to our need for God.

HERE'S THE POINT

Let's review, guys. The question, What are you thinking about? is really a question of, Are you thinking about *us*? Here's what you need to be thinking about when a woman shoots this question at you:

1. Even when you're thinking about nothing, she is usually thinking about something.
2. It's not a bad idea to start thinking about something besides

food, sex, and money. Think about the woman asking the question. Think about what we said would drive her to even ask the question.

3. Think about what she is wanting to hear in your answer to the question. Use the question as an opportunity to bless her and to speak to her longings and her desires.

And last, but certainly not least, remember that her brain may be smaller, but you're twice as slow as she is.

5
"AM I LIKE MY MOTHER?"

LET ME (STEPHEN) make it clear that both my wife and mother-in-law have read and approved this chapter. Second, let me say that they love, respect, and care for each other very much. With those important caveats, I write this: Though they have a wonderful relationship, my mother-in-law is second only to me when it comes to being able to wound and provoke my wife.

Over the years, seemingly insignificant remarks such as, "Your hair looks so beautiful long" (said right after my wife got her hair cut short); or the closely related, "You could stand a little more lipstick"; or the call to remind my wife to "make sure to be careful with the kids while you're at the mall" can send Heather over the edge. But none of this can be outdone by the atomic bomb of mother critiques, "That's not how I would do it, but you are free to do it however you like."

Sometimes, Heather will be talking to her mom on the phone, chatting away, when all of a sudden she is off the phone, aggravated: "I don't understand why she does that!" It's like my mother-in-law has some kind of mystical power over my wife with even the slightest of disapproving words. But the weirdest thing is that Heather and her mom are a lot more alike than different.

This became really clear one night a few weeks back. Heather and I were trying to decide if she was going to join me on a trip I was taking to the West Coast. I was going to a workshop in Seattle over a long weekend and thought it would be a great chance for Heather to get some time off from her responsibilities as a mother and domestic goddess. Everything would be paid for except her air-fare and meals. She would get five uninterrupted days of rest from parenting four children (ages six and under) and some needed time off from managing the affairs of our house—no interrupted sleep, no meals to fix, no bottoms to wipe, no bills to pay. What could be better? My plan was that while I attended the conference, Heather could sleep late or sightsee or do whatever she wanted to do. To me it was a no-brainer; Heather wasn't so sure.

The maternal part of her was apprehensive about the logistics of being away from our children for so many days. Her questions were legitimate: "Who is going to keep the kids?" "Will we split them up?" "We've never been gone together from them that long. Will they be okay?" With each concern I did my best to cajole, coax, reassure, and encourage her by offering solutions for her apprehensions.

"If you want, you can fly out a day later so you won't be gone so long," I offered.

"No. I don't like flying by myself."

"Heather," I began dismissingly, "how many times have you flown across the country by yourself? Ten? Fifteen? Twenty?" The conversation was beginning to go downhill. I could feel myself growing more irritated, and I could see her becoming more defensive.

"I wasn't alone," she said. "I had Emma Claire with me." (When we lived on the West Coast, Heather made numerous trips back to Tennessee with our then–baby daughter to visit family.)

"Emma Claire was a baby," I said in disbelief. I could feel myself going over the edge, so I attempted to reel myself back in and try to offer a solution. "What if she came with us? Would that be better?" This was a sincere offer.

"Yes, but . . ." she said. Heather's guilty grin exposed the lunacy in my own reasoning.

". . . how can a six-year-old keep you safe?" I said, finishing her sentence for her.

"She can't. I've just never flown alone. It makes me nervous, okay?"

"So why don't you fly with me?" I was getting more and more confused (and more and more belligerent).

That's when Heather came out with, "But what if we die in a plane crash?"

"Honey," I calmly and condescendingly began, "the chances of us dying in a plane crash are far less than us dying in a car wreck on the way to the store."

"My head knows that but I also know it could happen. I don't want our children to grow up without parents."

Now what had begun as playful banter was growing into a fight. I had little appreciation for my wife's existential angst.

"Heather, if you think by you staying here with the kids that it will keep anything bad from happening, you know you're wrong."

"I know that. But it still scares me."

"So let me get this straight. It's not okay if you and I die together in a fiery crash, but if you, our six-year-old daughter, and I plummet to our deaths, that's somehow better?" Now I was just being mean. I was anything but compassionate, and she could tell.

"I know what you're thinking," she said.

"Tell me. What am I thinking?"

"You're thinking that I am being like my mother."

"I wasn't. But come to think of it, you are." (Heather's mom's ability to imagine the most tragic of circumstances, then work herself and everyone else into a panic is legendary in the family.)

"I am not like my mother."

THE DAUGHTER DOESN'T FALL FAR FROM THE OVARY

My wife and her mother aren't dissimilar from other mothers and daughters. To be honest, most women are ambivalent about their mothers. On one hand, they adore and admire their mothers, and on the other hand, they hold their mothers responsible for their own personality quirks and character defects. A comment that would be harmless coming from anyone else can be a knife in the back when it comes from a mother. As best-selling author Deborah Tannen puts it, "Mothers and daughters find in each other the source of great comfort but also of great pain. [They] talk to each other in better and worse ways than [they] talk to anyone else."[1]

As you begin to peel back the layers of how mothers and

daughters relate to each other, there are mysteries far too vast to explain. The mother-daughter bond is possibly the most foundational relationship in a woman's life, yet it somehow ends up being the relational equivalent of the Rubik's Cube. For even as "relational" as women are, not even their relational mojo can decipher the complexities of this most fundamental relationship. While men and women speak very different languages, mothers and daughters share the same tongue but continue to often misinterpret each other.

But one thing is certain: Women *do* and women *do not* want to be like their mothers. As women move into adulthood, they struggle to find equilibrium between intimacy and independence in relation to their mothers. That's why the question, Am I like my mother? is so tricky for guys to answer. Essentially what this question is getting at is a much more specific question, How did my mother bless me and curse me, and will you love me in spite of my baggage? In other words, Will you love who I am becoming as much as you loved who I was the day you met me (even if I *am* like my mother)?

We set out on life's trail determined to either *not* become our parents (if they were lousy ones) or become a better version of who they were (if they were decent parents). But somewhere along the road, we each wake up to realize what Proverbs 26:11, NIV, means when it says, "a dog returns to its vomit." We go back to what is familiar to us, even if it's irrational or unhealthy. We gravitate back toward what we know—the good and the bad. This has happened as long as children have been growing into adulthood.

It's why children of alcoholics grow up to marry addicts or move into highly codependent relationships. It's why girls who grew up with violence in their homes often end up in relationships with abusive men—even as much as they hated the violence growing up. We are as predictable as trained lab rats in some of our behavior.

For some women, the question, Am I like my mother? is birthed out of a tendency to be with guys who are emotionally and spiritually more boys than men. Our culture is full of grown men who move into relationships with women because they want somebody to take care of them—to be their mommy. Likewise, there are women who prefer to be caretakers over having to emotionally rely on the strength of a man. It's like two puzzle pieces that fit together perfectly. A man who needs a mommy, and a woman who wants to be one.

Often men don't *need* a mother as much as they just *want* another one. We call it the Prince Mentality: someone to take care of them, tend to them, and be available to meet their needs. It's how they come to understand the role of a spouse.

BEING SCOLDED BY MOMMY . . . I MEAN MY WIFE

My (David's) kids have been asking for some Crocs lately. I didn't even know what they were until someone educated me. Crocs are (expensive) plastic, slip-on shoes with holes in them and a picture of a crocodile on both sides. They are the shape of a Dutch wooden shoe and look like they were made for gardening. And they evidently have some orthopedic value, although I'm not sure what that is. Every kid we know has some; therefore, my kids have been begging for their own.

There was enough conversation about these little plastic

shoes that I finally agreed to take a look at what all the fuss was about one Sunday afternoon. We packed everyone into my wife's Expedition and headed out for an early dinner and a trip to the shoe store that was rumored to have every color of Crocs that ever came off the manufacturing line—fuschia, lime, sea blue, bright yellow, chocolate . . . you name it, they had it. As we pulled into the strip mall, I caught site of a parking space on the front row outside the Crocs store. I opted to back in and let the kids jump out on the driver's side.

I am a master at sliding my wife's enormous vehicle tightly into small spaces. However, this time, just as I was about to put the car in park, I felt a slight bump and rub. I looked into the rearview mirror and saw nothing. My wife looked at me with a "What was that?" expression on her face. Then she hopped out to investigate.

She had no sooner walked around the back of our monster vehicle when I heard these words: "Oh, David, get out and come here quick." I shifted the car into drive, edged forward slightly, put it into park, and jumped out to explore what had elicited such a dramatic reaction. Behind me was a brand-new white 2007 Porsche 911 Carrera S Cabriolet. The car looked as if it had spent an hour of its life (at most) off the lot. And in its short lifespan, it had only been washed, waxed, admired, caressed, worshipped, stroked, coveted by others, and driven to this parking space. I didn't see any visible markings on its perfect paint job from where I stood and immediately challenged my wife on her exaggerated response. Her rebuke was merely, "Well, come over to this side and take a look."

I walked around the Expedition to observe two quarter-size

dents where the bumper looked pressed in. It resembled the plastic lid on a fountain drink where they press in the Diet, Sprite, or Tea options. There was no damage to the paint job, but the pressed-in spots were somewhat obvious. You had to look at just the right angle, but you could see them. I reluctantly looked around to see if I could identify the owner (an extremely wealthy man or woman, someone crying in hysteria at this sight or seething with rage). I didn't see either.

By this point, the kids were climbing out of the car and witnessing all the theatrics, so I instructed Connie to head into the store while I did a little crisis management. She stood paralyzed for a moment and then turned to head toward the kids. She had no sooner taken a step when she spun back around and launched into a hostile critique of my parking strategies.

"You *always* choose the closest spot. It's like a game to you, isn't it? Just circling the lot waiting for the closest spot and then you try and cram this enormous vehicle into some compact space made for a sedan. It's ridiculous, and here's a perfect example of what can happen." She paused (just long enough to catch her breath) and then started back. "Look at this parking lot. Do you see how many other options you had? You just hit a Porsche, David . . . a brand new Porsche! I cannot imagine what this is going to do to our insurance premium." I looked at her and said nothing. I am certain I looked like a scolded child, and I was sort of hopeful she felt plagued with guilt for lecturing me like a nine-year-old.

When I did respond, I simply said, "Why don't you just take the kids inside and let me deal with this." Breathing heavily, she corralled our children, crossed over to the sidewalk, and headed for the shoes. I stood there surveying the damage, reeling from her tongue lashing and reluctantly looking for the owner. Part of me hoped the owner would emerge. The other part of me did *not* want to encounter this individual.

I'll confess that half of me wanted to start my engine, quickly move my SUV to the other side of the parking lot, and hide out in the Crocs store until the storm blew over, never being linked to the crime at hand. *No one saw me do it. It's two stinking little dents that I could likely pop out myself with a hammer, a dish towel, and five minutes alone. Besides, paying for two dents on this car will involve sacrificing all three of my kids' college funds.* I sparred for a good five minutes with the voices in my head.

Around that time, I looked across the parking lot and saw my daughter standing against the glass of the store, watching this scene. I stood hostage in the opportunity I had been given to teach something to these little people that watch my every move—my children. Even then, I wanted to run across the sidewalk and instruct, "Okay, kids, here's the deal. If you should ever hit a tiny sports car like this, get out of Dodge, because you'll never recover from the insurance penalty. Run! Run! Run! Forget that garbage they teach you in Driver's Ed." Instead, I pulled a piece of scrap paper from the glove box and wrote the following note:

> Dear Sir or Madam,
>
> I regret to inform you that when backing into my spot, I bumped the front of your vehicle. I apologize and would like to take responsibility. Please contact me at the number below, and I'll touch base with my insurance company regarding reimbursement for the damage.

I signed my name, put my cell number, tucked it under the windshield, and headed in to buy the expensive plastic gardening shoes. Half an hour later, my kids emerged from the store, freshly fitted, skipping down the sidewalk with new Crocs on their feet. I noticed the note still tucked under the wiper as I loaded everyone into the car. I thought to myself, *Kids, these are going to be the most expensive shoes I ever put on your feet. I could have flown to Australia, traveled deep into the Outback, speared and skinned a live crocodile, and handmade real croc shoes for the three of you and a handbag for your mother. We will never recover financially.*

I shoved that thought to the back of my head and used the drive to dialogue with the kids about integrity and honesty. I talked with them about the note, and they asked a lot of questions. One of my sons asked, "When will the Porsche man call and tell us how much it costs to fix the car?" I thought to myself, *I hope never. Maybe the note will blow off the windshield.* Instead, I answered by saying, "When they come out of whatever store they were in and see the note I left for them." *They'll get wildly hysterical.* "Then they'll call."

Not even fifteen minutes had passed when the phone rang. It was a gentleman, *a very angry gentleman*, the owner of a 2007 White Porsche 911 Carrera S Cabriolet. He introduced himself and then informed me that "this was one of the worst days" of his life. I apologized for what had taken place and reassured him that I would take responsibility for the damage.

He informed me that he would be taking the car to a dealership in Florida where he had purchased the Porsche (and where he had a second home). He didn't trust anyone else with his cars.

Once he received a quote, he would immediately fax it to me. I kindly agreed to his strategy. He didn't end there, though. He went on to educate me that the car was brand new and had a price tag of one hundred thousand dollars.

He continued by asking, "Do you have *any* idea what it will cost if any *part* of the 911 Carrera S Cabriolet has to be *replaced*?" I was doing okay with his anger (and his insane self-absorption) until that question. It just didn't sit well with me. I responded by assuring Daddy Warbucks that I imagined the bumper on the 911 Carrera S Cabriolet would cost more than my entire SUV, and I might have to sell one of my three kids on eBay to get the kind of cash I would need.

He didn't think that was funny at all, jumped right over my sarcasm, and abruptly shifted into education on Porsche production and repair. He was extremely knowledgeable because he had owned several in the past and currently owned two. He kept one at his house here in Nashville and one parked at his residence in Florida.

By this point in the conversation, I was moving from remorse to anger of my own. I found myself having thoughts like, *What in the world would possess you to buy a hundred thousand dollar car in the first place? Are you not aware that millions of children are starving across the world and thousands are dying in Africa? Do you know how many Habitat for Humanity houses you can build with a hundred grand? For that amount of money, I could send all three of my kids to state universities, buy each of them a used car, and still contribute to my favorite non-profit organizations*. I considered sharing these thoughts with my new friend, but something in me just knew it wouldn't go over well.

Instead, I pulled one of my therapist tricks out of the bag. I began reframing his emotion with the goal of diffusing his anger (and shutting him up). "I can tell that you are angry about the damage *(Mr. Narcissism),* and again I want to reassure you that I have every intention of covering the damage. Just send me the estimate you receive *(from your rich, dishonest, money-sucking Porsche dealer in Florida, five blocks from your vacation home, you pompous son of a gun),* and I'll be glad to take care of it."

I said it in my most compassionate therapist voice and did indeed shut him down. He said, "You'll be hearing from me in seven to ten days." We ended our call, my wife standing nearby awaiting the state of the union address. I gave her the condensed version and ended with this statement: "I already feel lousy about this, and we're probably going to have to sell one of the kids to pay for the bumper on the 911 Carrera S Cabriolet. Please don't heap any more guilt or condemnation onto what's already there."

She looked at me and said, "I'm sorry, David, I'm really sorry. I lost it in the parking lot. Did I really turn into my mother back there?" I nodded in agreement without saying a word. I didn't need to say a word. She was standing knee deep in the awareness of what she had walked into. (And I thought I'd let her wade there for a moment.)

She simply said, "I'm sorry and I should have never said what I did. I don't want to act like I'm your mother." That night, as we climbed into bed, she brought it up again. And she again asked for forgiveness. Her words stayed with me as I lay awake in the dark doing the math in my head. I brainstormed over second mortgages, selling the car and biking to work, going back to Ben & Jerry's to discuss weekend shifts, etc.

Connie was very obviously doing some thinking of her own. She rolled over and asked, "Do you think I'm like my mother?" I remember thinking in my mind, *You cannot ask me a loaded question like that at midnight after I've just hit a Porsche. You just can't do this to me, honey. Don't ask me to walk across a minefield when I've just blown up the Sultan's motorcade.*

"Listen, Connie, it's not a good idea for us to go *that* deep *this* late and following *this* day." She agreed and we ended the discussion there. The next day (as is *always* the case with a woman), she revisited our late-night pillow talk. I realized, as our conversation unfolded, that my wife wasn't *really* asking about her mother. Or my mother. Or treating me like I'm her fourth child. She was *really* asking, "Will you love me in spite of my baggage?"

Because the truth lies here. My mother-in-law is an extraordinary woman. She raised two kids while working fulltime as a teacher. At one point when my wife was young, my father-in-law took a job that required his living out of town Monday through Friday, driving home to be with his family for the weekends. He made a great sacrifice to provide for his family. His wife made an enormous sacrifice to, in essence, become a working, full-time single parent during the week. It was a hard season from how they describe it, and I'm certain no one was at their best.

So the question, for my wife anyway, was not, Am I like this awful person? Her mother certainly has her shortcomings, but we all do. The question was *really*, Do you love me in spite of all the junk I bring into this relationship? Will you forgive me when I flip into acting like I'm the parent and you're a nine-year-old boy in some kind of trouble?

IN COMES MR. MAN

The mother-daughter relationship is the toughest relationship to reconcile and come to terms with in the lives of many adult women (both as mothers and as daughters). If a woman is to have peace with her own identity, she must find peace with the guilt and resentment she feels toward her own mother or daughter. And this is where a guy can help.

How? Glad you asked. If we are to love the woman in our life well, we will help her reconcile who she is as a woman with and without her mother. The primary role a man can play is that of an intimate ally. As her ally, he can support her while she explores her story by encouraging her to talk with other women who can help her better understand some of the dynamics of her mother-daughter relationship (this may even be a therapist). As she wrestles with how to love her mother and herself better, he can talk with her and listen to her about what she is coming to understand, without offering any advice.

Another way he can be her ally is not to throw her mother back in her face. One of the most cutting remarks any man can make to a woman is to disparage either her or her mother—no matter how whacked her mom may be. He can support the woman in his life by honoring her mother.

As her ally he can defend her from her own harm by helping her love herself and her mother better. This is particularly important if he is a husband and/or a father. He can intervene with strength and kindness between his wife and daughter (or wife and mother) when they are at war and keep them from damaging their relationship.

Finally, as an ally he can help cast a vision for what the mother-daughter relationship can become. The scriptures offer an excellent picture of this in the Old Testament book of Ruth. This short narrative of a woman (Naomi) and her daughter-in-law (Ruth) gives us a picture of what it means for a woman to reconcile the simultaneous virtues and failings of a mother. The story goes like this. . . .

A really, really long time ago—when Israel was being led by warriors—there was a famine, so there was little food. A Jewish man from Bethlehem named Elimelech took his wife, Naomi, and his two sons and headed for another country called Moab. For a Jew, Moab was a morally tough place to live. It would be kind of like Billy Graham moving his family to Las Vegas. Once in Moab, Elimelech died, and his sons married some locals named Orpah and Ruth. Then the sons died.

Now, women in this time had no social standing or identity outside of their husbands and fathers, so Naomi and her two daughters-in-law were lost. Naomi needed a plan so she decided to leave Moab and head back to Bethlehem—especially after hearing that there was food in Israel. Naomi, Orpah, and Ruth hit the road.

It wasn't long into the trip that Naomi told her daughters-in-law, "Go back. Go home and live with your mothers and find new husbands." Full of self-pity and disappointment, she kissed them, and they all cried together. That's when the girls said, "No, we're going on with you to your people." This is when Naomi's pity party got going in full swing.

> But Naomi said, "Return home, my daughters. Why would you come with me? Am I going to have any more sons,

> who could become your husbands? Return home, my
> daughters; I am too old to have another husband. Even
> if I thought there was still hope for me—even if I had a
> husband tonight and then gave birth to sons—would you
> wait until they grew up? Would you remain unmarried for
> them? No, my daughters. It is more bitter for me than for
> you, because the LORD's hand has gone out against me!"[2]

And they cried together again (they were women after all). Orpah
kissed her mother-in-law good-bye, but Ruth insisted on staying
with Naomi. Naomi said to her, "Look, Orpah has gone back to
Moab and to her gods. You should do the same."

> But Ruth replied, "Don't urge me to leave you or to turn
> back from you. Where you go I will go, and where you
> stay I will stay. Your people will be my people and your
> God my God. Where you die I will die, and there I will be
> buried. May the LORD deal with me, be it ever so severely,
> if anything but death separates you and me." When Naomi
> realized that Ruth was determined to go with her, she
> stopped urging her.[3]

When Naomi figured out that Ruth wouldn't change her mind,
she stopped trying to convince her. The two of them continued on
their road trip. When they finally arrived in Bethlehem, the entire
town started talking. The women in the town asked, "Is it really
Naomi?" (Which is a nice way of saying, "She looks like crap.")

True to form, Naomi's response was more self-pity and
resentment. "Don't call me Naomi," she told them. "Call me Mara

(which means bitter), because the Almighty has made my life very bitter. I went away full, but the LORD has brought me back empty."[4]

Excuse me! Hey, Naomi! You're not empty. You have a daughter-in-law who loves you more than her own mother. She just walked across the desert with you, left all she knows to stand in your corner. She has cried with you and been your friend. Orpah was hesitant to part from you; yet she did not love you enough to leave Moab. Ruth's resolution in the face of your bitterness, resentment, and negativity is akin to a daughter choosing to accept and love a difficult mother.

Often we hear preachers talk of Boaz as the hero of this story (he is usually referred to as a Christ figure). This is certainly very true. Boaz's role as redemptive figure is powerful and points us towards Christ. What is often overlooked, however, is how much Ruth gives us a picture of Christlikeness. Though Boaz is heralded as the champion of the story, Ruth is for sure our unsung hero, the suffering servant. Boaz is kind, protective, and obedient. He fulfills his responsibility with nobility and kindness. Ruth goes beyond what is required and chooses a quiet way of sacrificial love that ultimately changes the character of Naomi from bitter to peaceful in the end.

Boaz marries Ruth, and she gets pregnant and has a son named Obed (Jesus' great-great-great-great-great-grandpa). Naomi takes care of the baby like he's her own son. "The women said to Naomi: 'Praise be to the LORD, who this day has not left you without a kinsman-redeemer. May he become famous throughout Israel! He will renew your life and sustain you in your old age.

For your daughter-in-law, who loves you and who is better to you than seven sons, has given him birth.'"[5]

Ruth paints a great picture of how to love a difficult mother. What does it mean for a daughter to honor her mother? It means to see in her mother more than her mother sees in herself. It means to stand in the presence of verbal jabs (intended or not) and choose to confront them with love. "Am I like my mother?" In many ways, Ruth was and she wasn't. Like Naomi, she never forgot God. But unlike Naomi, Ruth chose to rise above being like her mother-in-law. She rejected Naomi's resentment and bitterness and instead put hope in God that he would restore them. And he did.

HERE'S THE POINT

The question of, Am I like my mother? is really, Will you love me in spite of my baggage? Your job is to love her in spite of the junk she brings into the relationship (because you bring your own junk) and to help her unpack it. You can do that by functioning as her ally.

1. Support her while she explores her story. Be a safe place while she unpacks her own pain, heartache, and disappointment.
2. Honor her mother. Regardless of what you experience with her, she is the woman who mothered the woman you love.
3. Defend her. It's your job to stand in harm's way when it comes to the woman you love. That may mean protecting her from her own mother, her own children, or even herself.
4. Cast a vision for her of how the relationship could look different—how it could be something more, something deeper and more holy.

6
"ARE YOU AS HAPPY AS I AM?"

ONE OF MY (David's) four-year-old twin sons has an enormous crush on my wife. About a month ago at breakfast, he informed the family, "Me and Mommy are getting married when I get bigger." He looked extremely disappointed when I told him that even though Mommy doesn't like it when Daddy drives too fast on the interstate, she is planning to stay married to me for the rest of her life, and he would need to find someone else to marry when he got bigger.

A month later, he is still wrestling with that news and has decided to stop calling my wife Mommy, affectionately referring to her as "Sweetie" or "my Sweetie." It began one Sunday evening, when we were putting our kids to bed. He looked her in the eyes, cradled her face in his little hands, and said, "Goodnight,

Sweetie." We couldn't help but break into laughter when he said it. When we retired downstairs, I looked over at my wife and asked, "Did he really just call you 'Sweetie'?" She nodded and smiled, the way a mother smiles when one of her children can't contain the affection he has for her.

So, now I'm Daddy, and I'm married to his mother, Sweetie. (I'm getting a lot of mileage out of his infatuation.) Sometimes, when Connie and I are both exhausted—the kitchen is filthy, the kids need a bath, and we're taking dibs on who gets the bedtime ritual—we do rock, paper, scissors. When my wife chooses paper and I choose scissors, my son smiles with enormous pleasure because his mother is officially on duty. I'll simply look her way and say, "It's tough work being 'my Sweetie,' but somebody's gotta do it."

My wife is trying to ride the Sweetie Train for as long as she can, because she knows the ride will come to a halt at some point soon and she'll be asked to disembark from the train. I've been teaching a class on male development for about six years, and my wife took the class for the first time last year. She commented to me that her least favorite part of the class was the section on how boys psychologically separate from their mothers and how important this is to their overall development. As I spoke about the separation, I caught my wife's eyes, and she had this look of pain and anguish across her face, like someone had just punched her in the stomach and walked away.

DUCK, DUCK, GOOSE

My wife knows the Sweetie Train is a short ride in the big scheme of things. She understands this just as I understand there will come a day when another man will capture my daughter's attention. For now, however, I'm *the man*. She is still pretty oblivious to the attention and affection of other males. I saw this for the first time when my daughter was three.

We went for a parent-teacher conference with her preschool teachers. Our conversation graduated from a discussion of her academic performance to her social development. Her teacher commented that a boy in Lily's class had become infatuated with her, and she was having some difficulty developing relationships with the other kids because this boy would attempt to sit by her at *every* lunch, follow her from station to station acting like Jim Carrey on steroids, pretend to be a superhero on the playground by circling her, and even plow down their classmates just to stand next to her in line, making strange noises to gain her attention.

I'll give the kid this much—he's got great taste. I know I'm biased, but other adults have confirmed that my little girl is indeed a knockout. She is tall and delicate, built like a ballerina with fair, porcelain skin and long blonde hair that falls across her little face. Lily has deep green eyes and a quiet, gentle spirit. Her admirer, on the other hand, was the shortest guy in the class. He had crazy, blond curly hair that stuck out in every direction. He looked like a white, three-year-old version of Lenny Kravitz, minus the tattoos and nose ring. When I observed him in the classroom, I think the kid might have had some attention issues. He was all over the map—the guy was wild and *full* throttle.

So here's Lenny Kravitz, plowing down innocent bystanders in pursuit of my little girl. I asked the teacher, "What does she do with his attention?" She decisively remarked, "Honestly, David, I think she ignores him much of the time. He follows her around, doing all this crazy stuff to try and get noticed, and I'm not even certain she's always aware that he is in the room or working so hard to capture her attention." I smiled and said, "Yes!" under my breath as I continued trying to appear to be a well-informed, curious, developmentally minded, academically concerned parent at a conference. At dinner that night I casually brought up Lenny.

"Lily, we met with Miss Wendy today, and we loved hearing her tell stories about what a delight you are to have in class."

She smiled and continued eating her PB and J.

"She said you have so many friends in your class like Emma Claire, Sadie, Jake, and Lenny."

She looked up for a split second with jelly oozing from her bottom lip.

"Now I know Emma Claire really well and I remember meeting Sadie and Jake the first day, but I can't really remember that other boy. What is he like?"

She answered without even thinking, "He's the one with crazy hair. And sometimes he follows me around too much."

I immediately moved into her words. "You don't like it when he follows you around?"

She put down her sandwich and casually said, "No. But I *do* like that he always picks me in Duck, Duck, Goose. He picks me *every* time and no one else."

Later that night, I reflected on my daughter's words and the game of Duck, Duck, Goose. You remember the rules? One person is it. This person walks slowly in a circle gently tapping (unless you're a boy) other participants on the head naming "duck" until someone is chosen by yelling "goose." At this point, the "goose" begins running around the circle in hopes of catching the tapper before he or she makes it to the seat where the "goose" was sitting. Then it repeats itself. So what is it about this game that made it an okay context for Lenny's antics?

I believe there's something about this game that speaks well to the design of men and women and the interplay between the sexes. First of all, I believe men were designed to pursue—to initiate, to hunt, to chase after with intention, courage, and strength. There really is something in the heart of a woman that longs to be chosen and pursued, to be invited into the process and bring her strength and beauty to bear. Even at three, my little girl experienced some kind of thrill when she was picked and chased. When Lenny stopped bouncing off the walls and shed his attempts at entertaining her, she noticed his attention in choosing her.

For a woman, the desire to be chosen is woven throughout all her relationships. As we stated before, it's where women and girls punish and hurt one another in the context of relationship. Exclusion is the sword a woman draws. The place where a woman feels most chosen is also the place where she experiences the most wounding. Just peek in on the play between elementary school girls. Watch them invite one another in and then turn and exclude someone in the same exchange.

Equally so, the material we explored around the power of a mother's role in a woman's life can be every bit as damaging. Women who have been wounded by other women is a category in itself. If you've ever had the opportunity to watch two cats go at each other, it wouldn't surprise you to know why women are described as being "catty" with one another.

Now, factor relationships with men into this concept of acceptance and exclusion. Think about it. How many women do you know who were abandoned as a girl by their fathers? Maybe he left for another woman, for work, or for an addiction. It's a deep, deep wound. How many women do you know who were abandoned by a boyfriend or husband in a similar way? It cuts deep.

One of my (Stephen) favorite movies is *She's Having a Baby* by John Hughes. It's about high-school sweethearts turned newlyweds Jake and Kristy Briggs. Jake (Kevin Bacon) is a bit less prepared than Kristy (Elizabeth McGovern) for the full reality of marriage and all that it (and his parents and in-laws) expects from him.

Jake faces the typical ups and downs of any new marriage, new job, and the ambivalences of being in his midtwenties. He is wondering if married life is all it's cracked up to be. Does he want children? Is there *life* in the suburbs? Will his career be satisfying?

One disastrous night after both sets of parents have come for dinner, Kristy and Jake are lying in bed talking.

Kristy: If I tell you something, will you promise to not get mad?

Jake: What is it?

Kristy: Promise you won't get mad?

Jake: Tell me what it is.

Kristy: You have to promise not to get mad.

Jake: Okay. I promise I won't get mad.

Kristy: I stopped taking the pill three months ago.

Jake: Aah! [*Jake envisions himself strapped in a seat flying into a wall.*]

Overwhelmed by doubts, unfulfilled ambitions, and images of a fantasy girl, Jake's not sure of the idea of parenthood. When Jake learns that he has a low sperm count, he feels like his manhood is disgraced. Then when he reluctantly comes on board, he and Kristy try and try for several months to get pregnant. They endure fertility treatments, monitoring her temperature religiously, and practicing conception-friendly positions. As a man, Jake is sucking wind.

One morning, as Jake is coming into the office, he is stopped by the receptionist, who tells him that his wife called, and she wants to meet him downtown at 5:00 p.m. at the Museum of Natural History. We find Jake walking slowly through the museum toward his wife. She is seated in front of a giant fountain looking at him. As he comes to her, she stands and stares into his eyes.

Kristy: Jake, we're going to have a baby.

Long pause, she smiles as she looks at him.

Kristy: I found out this morning, and I didn't want to tell you on the phone.

Another pause.

Kristy: How do you feel?

Jake is silent.

Kristy: Are you as happy as I am?

Jake: I think so . . . yeah. Yeah.

They embrace. The camera looks over her shoulder at Jake's face. His eyes are full of panic. The camera then shows her face. She is smiling with joy.

Kristy: We're blessed.

Jake just stares with fear.

Like with Kristy Briggs, the question, Are you as happy as I am? comes from women usually at times when they suspect the guy is not satisfied in the relationship. It's like a sonar beacon pinging into the relational depths looking for a returning signal.

For my wife, this question comes up when life is most crazy, like at the end of a day when all four kids have been crying and difficult, the phone wouldn't stop ringing, the house is in disarray, the bills need to be paid, and we both need a stiff drink. "Are you as happy as I am?" She's checking to see that I am still with her. That she still matters, and I have not planned some secret escape plan to a far-off island.

NUMERO UNO

The sum of it all is this: Acceptance and being chosen equate to contentment and happiness in a relationship. Abandonment and exclusion breed the opposite—discontentment and pain. So when a woman asks the question, Are you as happy as I am? on some level she is wrestling with these concepts. It's exactly what stirred excitement in Lily at three years of age. She *loved* being *chosen*. Out of every girl in the circle, he picked *her* (over and over and over). She loved being a *priority* in this young man's life.

That's what the loaded question is *really* about. It's what drives the question in the first place. Are you happy enough to still chase after me? Do you still choose me over every other person in the circle? And will you choose me over every other thing? Am I that kind of *priority* in your life? Will you choose me over work? Will you choose me over golf? Will you choose me over a night out with the guys? Will you choose our family over your own ambitions?

My wife and I (David) back into these kinds of questions again and again as our lives become more full and complex with things like three children, work, family, writing, creating a home, and relationships with friends. The list just goes on and on. She still longs to be chosen and chased by me, just as much as she wanted it when we met in college years ago. Out of every option available to me, I chose her.

She also longs to be chosen by our children. Therefore, she loves being Sweetie. Just as I am chasing after her, she is chasing after our children (both literally and figuratively). And she loves when they are chasing after her. The night she tucked my little boy into bed and his tiny hands formed the shape of her face and she first heard his new name for her (following his marriage proposal a week before), her heart was filled to overflowing. It's acceptance and contentment all over again.

FRUIT BASKET UPSET

But this is where it gets even more complex. Go back to the circle of Duck, Duck, Goose. Other than Lenny, most folks in the game are choosing one "goose" and then another. You are the "goose" (pursuer) in one moment of the game and the "duck" (the one being pursued) in the next. It's not that complicated.

For Connie and me, it all began with my pursuing her. I chose her and started running frantically after her. Once I caught her and captured her attention, she became equally interested in me and we traded back and forth in our own little romantic version of Duck, Duck, Goose. I chase her, she chases me. Back and forth. Beautiful.

However, early in our relationship, I began chasing after a graduate degree, in addition to this beautiful woman I had encountered. Connie began chasing a teaching career. For the most part, the game still centered on our pursuit of one another. Are you as happy as I am? wasn't so complicated a question at that point. Shortly after, I began chasing my career and building a practice at an agency that I loved. We bought an old house and started renovating it. We began chasing the dream of beginning a family and wound up pregnant. This is where the game changed drastically.

When my daughter was born, my wife began chasing after her. I felt a bit like the other kids in the circle must have felt when Lenny continued choosing Lily. My wife stopped choosing me for the game. Do you remember how it worked in some versions of Duck, Duck, Goose, where you got tagged and instead of getting to be it, you had to go to the middle of the circle and sit out a round while they referred to you as the "bad egg"? I felt like the bad egg. Once I came out of the circle, I, too, began chasing after my daughter. This pursuit of children is highly regarded in our culture, and while it looks nothing short of noble, it can be damaging when the kids become the center of the universe and their parents lose sight of their marriage. Families disintegrate every day because of this evolution.

So here's my wife chasing our daughter and all her dreams of family, being a mother, and creating a home, while I'm chasing our daughter and my career. Periodically we'd pause and chase one another again. We obviously caught each other at some point again in the game, because we somehow got pregnant again . . . this time with *twins*! (I eventually recommended we not play the game the same way—maybe we would only chase each other wearing extra protective gear.)

Now my wife is chasing after three children. Our kids are chasing after our attention. I'm chasing my kids and my career. I'm chasing a dream of writing. As a family we're chasing after relationships with friends, school, our families, soccer, church, and on and on and on. It looks less like Duck, Duck, Goose and more like Fruit Basket Upset. Everybody is running after something at the same time and it looks and feels chaotic.

This kind of chasing can breed chaos and discontentment. Nobody wins, and somebody always winds up getting hurt. It's the modern day family played out in a preschool game with no boundaries and no end in sight. It just goes on and on as new players are introduced into the game. My kids start chasing after new friends they meet, I chase new ventures vocationally, my wife chases after our chaotic life together as a family, my sons start chasing after girls and my daughter gets chased by boys (watch me get in the middle of that round), and eventually our kids chase a life of their own. They break away to find their own game involving players of their choosing. And unless we are extremely intentional throughout our life together, Connie and I lose sight of how to chase after one another the way we did in the earliest moments of the game.

Once the pursuit ends, she stops asking the question, Are you as happy as I am? because she knows the answer already or fears what it might be. Or she asks the question with anger and resentment, hurt, and years of disappointment. I turn away from the question because I don't know how to answer anymore. I don't even remember how to play with just her. I've chased after so many other things that have captured my heart in the absence of our pursuit.

WHO'S REALLY HAPPY, ANYWAY?

As a society, we're not really a very happy people. Only about 34 percent of American adults say that they're very happy.[1] Another half say they are "pretty happy" while 15 percent consider themselves "not too happy." This is not a new thing. These numbers have been pretty consistent since the 1970s. Some people are happier than others:

- Rich people (50 percent) are twice as likely to say they are happy as poor people (23 percent).
- People who worship every week (43 percent) are happier than those who never worship (26 percent).
- Republicans (45 percent) are happier than Democrats (30 percent) and Independents (29 percent).
- Whites (36 percent) and Hispanics (34 percent) are happier than African-Americans (28 percent).
- Thirtysomethings (36 percent) are no happier than seniors (38 percent) but both groups are happier than twentysomethings (28 percent).

- In terms of relationships, married people (43 percent) are far happier than single people (24 percent).
- Men (35 percent) and women (33 percent) are about equally as happy.

But is happiness really the point?

For many, it seems that creating a worthwhile relationship in today's fast-paced, career-focused, self-involved world is difficult. So, when you finally do find a soul mate, you want that relationship to *really* make you happy, right? It plays out this way. This guy and girl have been dating for some time. They are growing closer and closer and they get engaged and maybe even end up married. Somewhere in the process one or both of them start thinking, *How could this be Mr./Ms. Right when he/she makes me so frustrated?* They still have reservations and all the disappointing moments of past relationships, the toxic stuff passed on from their parents' marriages, and their own unrealistic expectations in their memories like a blooper reel on ESPN's *SportsCenter*.

Is true happiness and fulfillment even possible in a relationship? What makes a relationship work, anyway? What can anyone realistically expect in a romantic relationship? In our culture there is a lot of hope in finding the perfect mate. Doing relationship in a way that will deeply satisfy your need for authentic relational intimacy is a tricky business. Are some people just lucky? Or is there a way to better create relational intimacy and fulfillment?

THE BIG MYTHS

When it comes to that someone special, most people have an idea of their ideal type—tall, dark, and handsome; friendly, outgoing, and attractive; slim, blonde, and athletic. We all think we know what kind of person will fit our needs the most. There's the right mix of physical attractiveness, personality traits, and emotional stability. But we all know examples of the "perfect couple" who, to everyone's astonishment, broke up after years of being together.

Knowing what you want from a relationship is essential, but often we place unrealistic demands on what a relationship can be or do for us. We want things it was never intended to provide. We create these storybook wishes of what relationships can do for us (or not do for that matter).[2] These relational myths can destroy a relationship. There are many relational myths, but perhaps the two most pervasive are the Myth of Perfection and the Myth of Romance.

The Myth of Perfection says that the possibility of finding the "perfect" mate is realistic and desirable. This false belief tells us that if we just do all the right things, practice the right techniques, and get enough premarital counseling, our relationship will turn out the way we want. Often, with people who believe in this myth, you hear things like the following:

- "If we aren't fighting, everything is okay."
- "My mate should be able to meet all of my needs."
- "Finding the right person is the key to a good relationship."
- "Good communication can fix relationship problems."
- "Relationship is a fifty-fifty proposition."

This myth steals our joy by promising satisfaction that depends on mutual perfection. That is elusive and temporary. No one can meet another person's needs for long. The deeper the need, the more difficult it is for someone to satisfy.

The other popular myth is the Myth of Romance. This myth says that relationships are to be like fairy-tale romances. If there is enough romance, purity, or passion in the relationship, the relationship will be okay. Often this sounds like the following:

- "You must be married to have a fulfilling life."
- "If it's the right person, the relationship will be easy."
- "Love is what holds a relationship together."
- "When I find Mr./Ms. Right, everything will be okay."

This is probably the most pervasive myth out there. Absolutely, if two people delight in each other, there is great hope for the relationship, but this is only one of many ingredients in a recipe for a successful relationship. If you're looking for another person to fill the emptiness in your soul, you're asking for the impossible. Only the Father's love can fill up the cavernous recesses of the human heart.

Singer/songwriter David Wilcox speaks to these two myths in his song "Break in the Cup."[3] This song depicts the relationship between two people where their hope is that the love they share will fix all life's problems.

I try so hard to please you
To be the love that fills you up
I try to pour on sweet affection,
But I think you got a broken cup.
Because you can't believe I love you

> *I try to tell you that there is no doubt,*
> *But as soon as I fill you with all I've got*
> *That little break will let it run right out.*
> *I cannot make you happy.*
> *I'm learning love and money never do*
> *But I can pour myself out 'til I'm empty*
> *Trying to be just who you'd want me to.*

Later the song says

> *But now how could I still be so empty*
> *With all the love that you pour on me.*
> *I guess you cannot make me happy*
> *That's a money-back guarantee.*
> *But you can pour yourself out 'til you're empty*
> *Trying to be just who I'd want you to be.*

Your girlfriend, fiancée, or spouse is not a cure-all that will make your problems disappear. The truth is that no person (no matter how kind, caring, or well-intentioned he or she is) can fulfill another. No romantic love is durable, regardless of how passionately it burns.

There seems to be a general opinion, especially in Evangelical Christian circles (in which we authors work and live), that there is this one person out there that is perfect for us, and if we just find that person, then life will be okay. The Bible says it quite a bit differently. Scripture suggests that singleness for Christians is equally as good as marriage—even preferred. In 1 Corinthians 7, Paul writes:

Yes, it is good to live a celibate life. But because there is
so much sexual immorality, each man should have his
own wife, and each woman should have her own husband.
. . . I wish everyone were single, just as I am. But God
gives to some the gift of marriage, and to others the gift
of singleness.

So I say to those who aren't married and to widows—
it's better to stay unmarried, just as I am. But if they can't
control themselves, they should go ahead and marry. It's
better to marry than to burn with lust.[4]

This is a radical idea in much of popular Christian culture. Does
this mean that Paul is against marriage or that romantic love
is not a biblical concept? Not in the least. In fact, in Ephesians,
Paul writes how the love, loyalty, passion, and physical intimacy
experienced between a husband and wife is reflective of Jesus'
relationship with his people.[5] And in the wisdom literature of the
Old Testament, Song of Songs makes blatantly obvious the high
value that God places on the passion of betrothed lovers. Jesus
thinks so highly of marriage that he chose to begin his public
ministry at a wedding in Cana so that the party could keep on
going a little longer.[6] God is so into men and women doing life
together that this was the first relationship he fashioned.

But during the period of time when the Bible was written,
almost all marriages were arranged by the couple's parents (and
even today in some parts of the world this is still true). Mutual
fulfillment of each other and romantic love are not God's ultimate
hope for men and women—it's far, far grander than that.

Then what's God after? Well, it ain't your happiness.

HERE'S THE POINT

Take note, men. If you hear her asking if you're as happy in the relationship as she is, she's looking to see if she's safe and you're staying. She wants to know that she is a priority in your life. You can bring reassurance and hope to her heart.

1. Remember, women long to be pursued and chosen. She never stops wanting this—meaning you never stop bringing home flowers, sending her cards, and dating her.
2. Tell her that you're in. Remind her of your commitment to her—at whatever level of the relationship you're in at this moment.
3. Ask her what she needs. Seriously. Put this book down right now and ask her that question: Honey, what do you need from me? She will love you for this.
4. Take her to drink from a deeper well. Remember that God can make her far happier than you ever can.

And never forget that Duck, Duck, Goose is a much more complicated and strategic game than it appears on the surface.

7
"IS THERE ANYTHING YOU DON'T LIKE ABOUT ME?"

I (STEPHEN) DATED a woman (we'll call her Jane) in college for a short time. At first I really enjoyed my relationship with Jane. She was fun, attractive, intelligent, and had a great sense of humor. Then one weekend the wheels came off.

We went out to dinner at an Italian place not far from campus. The restaurant was crowded that night, but the candlelight and background music made the mood fairly romantic. Since the crowd was heavy and we were going to have to wait a while for a table, Jane suggested that we hang out in the bar area and get an appetizer. (Now, being a poor semi-employed college student, I didn't have a lot of money, and I hadn't been planning on appetizers, but what's a guy to do on a date, say no?) We slipped into one of the more private tables in the corner of the bar and prepared to order our appetizer.

"May I take your order?" the waiter asked.

"Do you want anything?" I asked Jane as the waiter stood patiently over our table.

"I think so," she answered and turned toward the waiter. "Are the mussels any good?" she asked.

"Oh, they're excellent. I think you'll be very pleased," he responded. "They are Prince Edward Island mussels, prepared in a garlic wine broth with diced tomatoes, capers, and grilled bruschetta."

"I'll have that," Jane said.

As she ordered, I was thinking to myself, *Mussels? You've got to be kidding me! Garlic wine broth? You might as well order a side of lobster tails and caviar to go with it.*

"Would you like a half order or a whole order, miss?" the waiter asked.

"I'm pretty hungry. You better make it a whole."

Noooo!

"And would you like that over angel hair for $2.00 more?"

Please. Stop! My hard-earned money!

"Oh, that sounds great. Yes, please."

The waiter turned to me, "And for you, sir?"

"Just water please," I said sternly while giving him a look that said, *Shut up. I'm broke. Now go away and never come back to this table.*

After a few moments, however, having emotionally and mentally recovered, I was able to regain some momentum in our conversation. A little shameless flirting here, a pretentious story from me there, and an obligatory laugh and hair toss from her to fill in the gaps. All in all, we were having a pretty good time—until the conversation began to turn toward my opinion of her. "Tell me what you think of me," Jane asked wryly.

I could tell that she was fishing, but I wasn't sure what she was looking for. A compliment maybe? An observation? A prophetic vision? I began by praising her great sense of humor and her laugh. I told her how beautiful her hair and eyes looked. I followed up with mentioning how intelligent she seemed. And, for good measure, I think I even worked in a comment about how much I liked her shoes. I finished my list of positive attributes feeling pretty good about myself for giving such a thorough answer. That's when Jane dropped, "Is there anything that you don't like about me?"

The question caught me so off guard that I just stared at her forehead with an expression that I'm sure looked as awkward as I felt. After a few too many seconds, I stuttered, "Uh-h-h-h, wh-h-h-h-at?"

Speaking to me as stupidly as I sounded, Jane answered me like I was some French-foreign-national who spoke English as a second language, repeating herself and slowly enunciating each syllable. "Is–there–an–y–thing–you–don't–like–a–bout–me?"

"Well. . ." I stalled. "From what I know of you, you're all right. You're all right. Yes, all right." I must have sounded like a cross between Forrest Gump and Rainman, because she promptly and politely excused herself to the restroom, and when she came back, she said that she had to work early the next day so we probably ought to just eat our appetizers and call it a night.

After several minutes of awkward conversation while she ingested far too few of her fifteen-dollar mussels with expensive garlic-something sauce on them, I took her back to her apartment, dropped her off at her door, and went on my way. As I drove, I realized that I never got to eat, so I went through Wendy's drive-through for a single with cheese while trying to figure out what went wrong.

Not surprisingly, we never went out again.

MATCHMAKING

A study published in the psychology journal *Current Psychology* revealed that women are generally more insecure than the men they want to date. The findings also revealed that women believe guys are more critical of them than the guys really are. The researchers discovered that there are significant differences in how women see themselves and their assumptions of what men are looking for in romantic partners.

Women rated themselves as being far less desirable than the men they want to date in a number of categories, including

- more unforgiving
- more overweight
- uglier
- more impatient
- more emotionally unstable
- dirtier and messier.

Generally this means that women look for men they feel inferior to in many categories. What's even more unusual is that women reported feeling like they didn't measure up to guys' expectations in the areas of appearance and kindheartedness. This means that when a woman finds the man of her dreams, her perception of herself is that of an overweight, ugly, unkempt, cold-hearted psycho—and she thinks he thinks that too.[1]

This is why the question, Is there anything you don't like about me? can be such a trap. Sometimes, when this question comes up, the woman is looking for the guy to tell her the "truth." Not the actual, factual truth, but what the woman believes to be true about herself.

That's the problem. Generally, men are not nearly as picky and critical of women as women are of themselves. And with women being more critical of themselves, they're not that likely to believe what he's saying anyway.

HEADS-UP!

A buddy of mine (David) told me a story of being asked for fashion advice from his wife, who, he has observed, unfortunately asks most wardrobe questions post-pregnancy. He commented to me that she has experienced a wide range of body configurations over the last six years and three pregnancies. He has tried to be sensitive to the emotional changes that accompany the physical changes, but on occasion, he has a lapse. Following the third pregnancy, his wife asked for his opinion about a particular outfit, a sleeveless shirt and a low-riding skirt. Unfortunately, this particular outfit didn't flatter her post-pregnancy shape at the time. He remembers noticing that the outfit made her top look very small and her bottom look very large (and no woman wants to look small in the upper torso and large in the lower).

He tried desperately to come up with a gentle, truthful way to comment on the outfit. However, he was sleep deprived from the baby and couldn't access the proper filter for his comments. He started with her arms. "Your arms will probably look better in that top in a few more weeks." She immediately responded with, "You think my arms are fat?" He never even got past the fat arms comment to give feedback on her lower half. He told me, "I did enough damage with just her arms to ruin the rest of the entire evening. I'm still not sure I've totally recovered. Sometimes she'll put on a top and ask how her 'fat arms' look in it." We agreed that unlike forgetting to put dishes in the dishwasher, it takes a long time to be forgiven for this kind of error.

Another buddy of mine told me that when his wife was fifteen weeks pregnant, she asked, "I'm not looking *too* pregnant, am I?" He was brutally honest and said, "Well, honey, you *are* getting a little thick in the waist." (I asked him what in the world he was thinking when he answered her that way.) He said he still wonders what he was thinking because she continues to talk about it five years later. This same friend said that another day his wife completely lost her cool with the kids. She looked at him moments after the gunfire subsided and asked, "I'm not too hard on the kids, am I?" He looked down at the ground and said, "Well, *I'm* a little afraid of you right now." She burst into a puddle of tears.

A third friend of mine said his wife will periodically ask him the question, Are you still glad you married me? But she only asks the question on a day when she hasn't had a shower and is covered with baby spit-up. He noted that she's usually sitting in the kitchen amidst a sea of dirty dishes, piles of laundry in the hallway, and the sounds of a temper tantrum in the background.

My own wife asked me a similar question in an almost identical moment. Pre-kids, my wife was one of the most emotionally stable women I had ever encountered. She was atypical in that, unlike most women who experience strong emotional bouts once a month like clockwork, I was clueless about my wife's cycle. I just never knew when it was her "time of the month." That was before children!

Following the birth of our first child, she had a severe round of postpartum depression. She was weepy for about eighteen to twenty of every twenty-four hours. (She slept the other four to six hours.) The relentless sadness shocked both of us, and it lasted for weeks and weeks after the delivery. Once it lifted, her emotions and her body seemed to evolve into a different kind of emotional and physical stability. I became keenly aware of her cycle.

Our second pregnancy involved carrying twins. It was double everything. Twice the car seats needed, two baby beds, a double stroller, two high chairs, a bigger house and a larger vehicle, twice as many OB appointments to track a high-risk pregnancy. I was fearful it might be double the emotions as well. When my wife got weepy in the pregnancy, I couldn't tell whether it was the double dose of hormones or just the reality of caring for a toddler while carrying twins. And this time around, instead of just being weepy, she would vacillate between being really sad and really irritable. She would yell things from the bedroom to the kitchen like, "Are you cooking fish in there? Something smells awful. Get rid of that smell." Or she would explode into a commentary on the house being too cold or too hot. "Get me a blanket. Quick! I'm freezing."

I walked into the house late one evening after work and found her sitting at the kitchen table surrounded by dirty plates, cold food, and cold pots on the stove. When I noticed she was crying, I immediately asked, "Honey, what's wrong?"

She wailed and said, "Nothing. Nothing in particular. Just everything. Everything in the world. This filthy house and my enormous stomach, my back is sore and my ankles have swollen, your daughter is so fussy, I have bills to pay, and I don't have the energy to clean up after dinner. So I've just been sitting here crying."

I surveyed the damage—the mounds of dirty dishes, the bills, my crying wife—and I imagined what life would be like after the pregnancy when we had *three* children under the age of three in our house. I wondered who would cry the most—one of the newborn twins, my daughter (whose life as an only child for almost two years would be completely disrupted), my wife (who, according to statistics, would likely have another, possibly worse bout of postpartum depression), or me.

And in that very moment, my *very* emotional wife looked at me and said, "Is there anything you don't like about me?" I remember thinking two things: one, *Maybe she's been drinking a little while she's pregnant.* (I looked around the kitchen for an empty wine bottle.) The second thought was, *Regardless of what I'm really thinking in response to that question right now, I should just say, "Not one thing, Connie, not one thing."* And that is *exactly* what I said.

The next morning we happened to have an ob-gyn appointment. We showed up at our doctor's office for our routine checkup and to talk about the delivery. We had delivered naturally with our first child and hoped to be able to do so the second time around. But our OB informed us that there could be a number of complications when delivering multiples. For example, the pressure involved with delivering Baby A can affect the heart rate of Baby B, resulting in a vaginal delivery of the first child and the need for a C-section with the second. Or the release of Baby A could shift Baby B into a breech or transverse position, again increasing the need for a C-section. With the conversation came the reality that my wife would need to be prepped for surgery, regardless of the outcome. We needed to be prepared for every possible scenario.

With this reality and the strong possibility of my wife being cut open during delivery, the conversation moved in a slightly different direction. The doc then said, "Women carrying multiples will, at times, consider the option of having their tubes tied while engaged in surgery." What I heard him saying was that you can get a 2-for-1 deal if a C-section is required. If your insides are already laid out on the operating table, just take care of any additional business at hand. Well, I thought that was about the best bargain I'd heard in a long time. Finally, the double everything phenomena would work in my favor! I sat straight up in my chair and said, "Tell me more." My wife looked over at me with a look of pure disgust and rage, and she responded with a definitive, "I understand why some women would consider that option, but I'm not interested!"

I made the enormous mistake of saying, "Well, Connie, can't we just hear the man out? Let's get all the information before we make a firm decision." At this moment, I am certain the doc wanted to excuse himself for a moment or run for shelter. He didn't utter a word and neither did my wife. She just looked straight at me with a look that seemed to say, *I will pretend I didn't hear a word you said.* (And she had this homicidal look about her. The fragile, broken woman from the kitchen the night before, who asked if there was anything I didn't like about her, was nowhere to be found).

INFORMATION VS. CONFIRMATION

The questions take so many forms. A woman looking at her body in clothes, a mother questioning her abilities after erupting at home, an adult daughter contemplating the similarities between herself and her mother, another woman staring at her face in the mirror.

> Do I look fat in this dress?
> Was I too harsh with the kids?
> How do my arms look in this blouse?
> Do you think that woman is pretty?
> Am I looking *too* pregnant?
> Did I sound ridiculous when I said that?
> How does this bathing suit work on me?
> Are you satisfied with this relationship?
> Can you tell that I've lost weight?
> Am I like my mother?
> Is this dress flattering on my hips?
> Did you like the chicken cooked that way?
> Do you like my hair this short?
> Are you still glad you married me?
> Will you give me your opinion on this outfit?
> Can you see the wrinkles forming around my eyes?
> Is there anything you don't like about me?

The essence of each of these questions is rooted in the deeper questions, Will you tell me the truth? Even if the truth hurts, will you love me enough to tell it to me anyway? Do you care enough about me to speak the truth in love?

BAGGAGE CLAIM

Why do so many women wrestle with their self-worth? How'd they lose it? Where did it go? Is it because of how women are portrayed in the media? Sure it is. Is it because they've been betrayed by someone they trusted? No doubt. Is it because they've been left to fend for themselves in a world that prefers men? Certainly.

Life is hard. We all (men and women) carry wounds and scars from life's heartaches. Those of us who have not done the work to resolve these hurts are condemned to suffer from them. In order to make life work the way we want it to, we develop coping skills and styles of relating that guard these wounds and still let us get most of what we need and some of what we want.

We're all familiar with the definition of crazy: doing the same thing and expecting different results. However, there are many of us who don't know how, or are too scared, or just plain refuse to make changes. This is especially true in relationships with men and women. The wounds that dictate our style of relating with others is commonly referred to as "baggage." It's called baggage because it weighs us down and keeps us from living in the fullness for which we were made. This is a way of relating that says, "I'm only as good as you think I am" or "as bad as I think I am."

Essentially, baggage is a standard of defining ourselves by "what I think you think of me." When we use this standard to define ourselves, we become trapped and cannot be who God created us to be. This way of relating causes us to try to manufacture and protect our own self-image. In the worst cases, this style of relating is debilitating and exhausting. It's a lose-lose situation. We don't really assume the best in others and let others see only the "best" of ourselves. It's the inner voice that may sound like this:

- I can't trust anyone.
- Everyone will let me down eventually.
- Why is it so hard to make friends (or get a date)?
- I need to look out for myself. No one really cares about me.
- I don't need counseling.
- It's not my fault.
- It's always my fault.

MY BAGGAGE IS HEAVIER THAN YOUR BAGGAGE

The truth is we are all messed up, we are all wounded, we let others down, and we all harm others (especially those we are closest to). No one is innocent. Women who put more faith in distrust and suspicion, who carry a list of others' offenses, will never know the joy of being chosen and loved by a noble man. Guys who are blind to their ego and self-centeredness will always miss experiencing a truly intimate and authentic relationship with a woman.

The natural tendency is to blame others or blame ourselves. The question, Is there anything you don't like about me? is too often a way a woman fulfills her own inward beliefs that she is not good enough, smart enough, or pretty enough. It's part of the human saga to look for our identity through the eyes of others.

The reality is, however, that our true identity comes from being stamped in the image of God—we bear his permanent likeness. It is not based on what we do. The good news is that God didn't wait for us to get our act together. He made the first move. His love is not dependent on anything we do or have done. His love is so deep, in fact, that he allowed his own Son to be killed so we could be with him forever. He is wild and passionate about us. The small responsibility we have is to acknowledge and accept that wild love and depend on it. The Bible says it this way:

> Even before he made the world, God loved us and chose us. . . . God decided in advance to adopt us into his own family by bringing us to himself through Jesus Christ. . . . And it gave him great pleasure.[2]

The Bible calls this God's "mysterious plan."[3] It's a plan centered on what Christ can do, not anything we have done or could ever do. Scripture speaks of how we are each wonderfully and marvelously made by God. And that God has precious thoughts about each of us—so many thoughts that they are like sand on the beach and cannot be counted.[4]

So, male or female, anytime we determine our identity or worth based on someone else or some standard of performance, we begin to create a vicious cycle that eats at our souls. Is there anything you don't like about me? can be a very helpful question in a relationship. It can also be a manipulative ploy to bolster or diminish another's self-worth.

WHO CAN'T HANDLE THE TRUTH?

Our guess is that a majority of the time, women already know the truth. They aren't asking for information as much as they are asking for confirmation. It may appear that you are the bearer of bad news, but oftentimes you're just the delivery guy. They already knew the package was scheduled to be delivered, but you're just showing up with the goods (or the bads, depending on the news). They want to see if you will speak the truth. This is the first level of confirmation a woman desires.

The second level of confirmation comes in the shape of commitment. The woman asking this question is wondering, *No matter what the truth is, will you stand in the reality of it with me? Regardless of the truth, will you stay with me? If my arms are fat or my hips are large, and this dress does anything but flatter me; if I sound like my mother or I lose my cool with the kids; if I burn the dinner for the sixth time and I can't bake like your mother; if I cry at the drop of a hat or I fly off the handle; if I sound like an idiot in front of your friends, or I embarrass you in front of your parents; if I can't stop gaining weight, and the house is trashed, the bills aren't paid, and I haven't even had a shower; are you still glad you met me? When my face begins to show the years I've lived and you think that woman is pretty, will you be faithful to the promise you made to me? When life is hard and our relationship is less than you imagined instead of more than you dreamed of, will you stay invested in what we have?*

The answer is a confirmation that speaks to the heart of a woman—a heart that longs for relationship. Angela Thomas, in her best-selling book, *Do You Think I'm Beautiful?* names this level of confirmation when she reminds us that "women ache for intimate connection. There is a desperate loneliness that settles on the heart not heard. Lonely for companionship. Lonely for expression. Lonely for affirmation."[5]

Will you tell the truth? A truth that calls men to integrity and honesty? A truth that calls men to commitment and promise? A truth that brings security and safety to a woman? Even when the truth hurts? Even when it sounds like "bad" news? That kind of truth, delivered by a man who carries a woman's heart with integrity, honesty, commitment, and promise, creates opportunity for healing, hope, challenge, change, and creativity.

HERE'S THE POINT

So guys, when you feel cornered by the words "Is there anything you don't like about me?" keep in mind that it's really a question of Will you tell me the truth? Even when the truth hurts, she wants you to shoot straight. You can do that by the following:

1. Targeting an honest but loving way to respond to her questions.
2. Remembering that God made women full of emotions and with hearts for relationships. And it is exactly as it should be. As much as that scares the heebie-jeebies out of us sometimes, we can move toward celebrating this.
3. Reminding her that her self-image and worth need to be in Christ, not in what you think of her. Ultimately, you are moving her back to the one whose "mysterious plan" was accomplished in the woman you love.

Conclusion
"YOU DON'T HAVE TO GET ME ANYTHING FOR CHRISTMAS."

I (DAVID) HAVE been married for more than a decade to the same woman, and she remains a mystery to me. However, you would think I might get some basic things down by this point in the game. Well, think again.

By the end of the first quarter, nearing halftime, you usually have a pretty good sense of who you're playing, the strategy of the game, the way they move the ball, their offensive and defensive strengths. Not me. I mean, I got a few things down, but doggone it if I don't make some of the same mistakes time and time and time again.

For example, my wife despises when I drive too fast on the interstate. We have some of our most explosive arguments over the way I handle a vehicle on the road. I know it's the quickest way to get a date night off on the wrong foot, yet I lose all sense of myself and turn into Mario Andretti behind the wheel, forgetting her not-so-gentle requests to "Stop speeding!"

One of my worst and most consistent mistakes surfaces every birthday and Christmas. In my family, we had a long-standing tradition of making lists for these two events. Around Thanksgiving, members of my family distributed a list of desired items among family members to guide the holiday shopping experience. Everyone did the same thing a month before their birthday. It's practical, cost-effective, and almost foolproof. It makes it easy on the gift giver, who doesn't have to spend hours, days, or weeks in search of the "perfect gift," and then spend the next hours, days, or weeks wondering if the recipient will like it or want to return it. I even write down the size, the title of the book, or where in the REI store you can find my desired items. Heck, I even provide a broad list of gift ideas covering a range of prices and convenience to particular retailers.

My wife thinks this is the kookiest idea she has ever heard. She rolls her eyes every time I provide her with "the list." She finds it lacking in creativity and absent of warmth and personalization. Sometimes I let her pick out whether to get a green shirt or a navy one, but that hasn't seemed to help. In her family, you didn't make requests. And despite my trying to meet somewhere in the middle, she refuses to give me any kind of list. She won't even provide me with broad categories like a sweater or something for the house. It drives me crazy. Almost as crazy as it makes me when she says (which she *always* does), "I really don't need a thing. You don't have to get me anything for Christmas."

But it doesn't end there. If I push her—I mean, really push

her for some ideas—she will most likely say something like, "You know what I love? It's when you plan for us to spend time together (which is a chapter in itself) and write something to me in a card." Okay, first of all, that is *so* wide open. I go into panic mode trying to find some activity that we can do together that would demonstrate how well I know her and what she loves to do. Second, we have some real issues around the card thing.

Here's my take on the greeting card scene: What a rip-off! Three bucks and fifty cents for a piece of paper with some words that will only get tossed in the garbage can, along with the wrapping paper, ten minutes after the birthday party. I'm of the mindset that you buy one box of blank stationery—nice hard stock paper is fine—and you use it for all occasions. Last year I even bought some with "The Thomas Family" written across the top in red letters. It worked for *every* occasion. "Merry Christmas, Mom and Dad" (with red for Christmas) and "Happy Valentine's Day, Sweetheart" (with red for Valentine's Day) and "Happy 4th of July" (with red letters and blue ink on the white card) and "Happy Birthday, Stephen" (red works fine for birthdays too). We send thank you notes on it, congratulations for weddings, hoorays for new babies. One card for all occasions.

Again, my wife thinks this is one of the strangest, most impersonal ideas she has encountered. She has supported the greeting card industry for years now. Really, we should have bought stock in Hallmark. Dozens of friends have received hundreds of cards for countless occasions from the Thomas family, and we've spent thousands of dollars over the years.

Because of our significant investment in the greeting card industry and my staunch beliefs in a uniform card for all occasions, it's painful for me to buy another flowery card and write all this mushy stuff to my wife when I just want a *list*. And furthermore, who doesn't want a gift? A really good gift—something *you've* been wanting. I believe everyone does, *including* my wife. I think she's just trying to trick me. *And I'm not falling for that again*, I think to myself.

So, I bypass her words and try and guess what gift she's *really* wanting. I think and think, poll her girlfriends, and then make the magical purchase. And at least eight out of ten times, she'll take it back to the store, swap it for something else, use the credit to buy something for the kids or the house, or stuff it in the back of her closet. At some point later (maybe that day or maybe a week or month later), after I voice my frustration at her displeasure over the gift, she will inevitably comment, "I told you I didn't need a thing" or "I told you that you didn't have to get me anything for Christmas" or "I told you all I wanted was a card." The truth is, I think she wants it *all*. She wants an experiential gift (doing something together that she loves, blah, blah, blah), a mushy, expensive greeting card, *and* a really good gift. I'm just sure this is the case.

WILL WE EVER LEARN?

Everywhere you look, men and women are stumbling through relationships. Much of the anxiety, pleasure, and confusion in life is tied to how one gender relates to the other. In this book, and its companion book, *"Yup." "Nope." "Maybe.",* we've explored how, through entering into the mysteries of the differences between women and men, we can find the fingerprints of God. By beginning to unlock some of the complexities of these relationships in your own life, we hope that you will now have more fulfilling and meaningful relationships.

In our work as counselors, we have witnessed how men and women trip all over each other. As husbands, we've experienced the complexity and richness and challenge of the male-female dynamic. But we have also felt the power of redeemed relationships and the transformation that takes place when one person is able to "find" another.

We've tried to humorously and authentically deal with the complexities of romantic love. By playing with some gross stereotypes, we've attempted to uncover deeper relational and spiritual realities. And along with the humor, we've tried to bring quite a bit of depth, insight, and credibility. This book examined some of the deeper themes behind the loaded questions that women use with men. We've offered some explanations to what the questions reveal about the women who ask them and the men who are confused by them.

After they read this book, we hope that women can ask much more vulnerable and honest questions and men can begin to give much more authentic answers. More than anything else, we wanted this book to guide men and women past the question of Why are we so different? to better see the glorious uniqueness of a God who shows himself in each gender.

How we view, interpret, and relate with the opposite sex says more about who we are than about who they are. Questions, especially loaded questions, reveal more about the one asking the question than they do about the one being asked. When it comes to a woman's loaded questions, they always lead back to some of her deepest desires and make known some of what she wants most from a man.

Men and women often desire different things from the same circumstance. What woman or man hasn't experienced a moment when one party thought that they were abundantly clear and the other totally heard something else? That's why we can never agree on a place to eat, a show to watch, or a color to paint. The plans of men and women are so different. Women are far more bent toward process—men far more toward movement.

So while almost every man has been caught in a woman's trap, very few men have had the tools to escape because they have never stopped to examine what is really being asked in the first place. Now you know.

AND THE WINNER IS . . .

Frustration, contempt, and despair are common experiences in relationships. If not, you wouldn't even be reading this book. No matter how well-matched a couple is (thanks, eHarmony), they will eventually fail each other. Every person is so unique that even the most like-minded and well-suited couple can provoke each other to sin. Always at competition in a relationship are happiness and holiness.

In relationships with the opposite sex, our transgressions against each other can be physical, emotional, psychological, and spiritual. No matter how hard we try not to, we will fail each other. Every day in a relationship, partners have the potential to let each other down, and the hard truth is that we will always struggle with this because of our sinful nature.

No matter how many books you read, counselors you see, prayers you pray, or marriage conferences you attend, you cannot escape the reality that you will hurt and harm the one you love at one time or another. Life is full of pain, and the majority of our pain in life comes from those we love the most.

Say it ain't so!

We wish we could. No matter how hard we try, we will harm each other in our relationships. If a man and woman spend an extended amount of time together, an offense will likely occur. For some couples, the first offense takes place early in their story; for others it happens somewhere down the road. But God will still use our hurts to shape us into the people that he longs for us to be, people who are becoming more and more like him. That's just how wildly he loves us.

He promises to love us and restore us and return us to our intended glory. But so much of our redemption this side of heaven as men and women is going to depend on how much suffering we are committed to endure on behalf of the ones we love.

As we wrote in *Becoming A Dad,* "[God] will comfort us, but He will never coddle us. He will engage us, but He will never manipulate us. He will provide for us more than what we ever could dream of, but He will never overindulge us. And whether we like it or not . . . maturity of the heart is synonymous with failure, pain, and powerlessness."[1] Is relationship hard? Oh, you bet! You must love well and with an open heart.

The question, especially for Christian men and women in relationships, shouldn't be, Are you happy? but rather, Does our love cause us to ache for each other's holiness? Do I fundamentally believe that God loves me more than you do? If this is the case, a man will be free to risk his happiness, security, and safety in the hopes that his woman will live more fully and freely.

God designed relationships, especially between men and women, as a place where our darkest sins will be revealed. It is a place where we can set down our baggage. It is also a place where we can step into maturity and discover that living fully means more than happiness, comfort, or thrills—it means having the capacity to experience true joy, while being equally capable of feeling true pain.

If you haven't figured it out yet, God designed relationships between men and women to have more failure than success.

IT'S ABOUT GOD'S GLORY, STUPID

God created relationships to be thrilling. God is writing your story so that you will be transformed and exposed in order to reveal his glory. He always uses the medium of dating and the institution of marriage to reclaim our hearts, our desires, and everything else in us. It's a means to some of the greatest pleasures and frustrations in life like you've never experienced. Women have the power to take men to some of the most glorious and uncomfortable places in life—and vice versa.

Relationships, at their best, drive us to greater surrender, create dependency on God, and uncover the unique image of God we each bear. God's design for relationships in general, and romantic relationships in particular, is sanctification. He is committed to setting his people apart and making us more mature, wise, and loving—more like himself. In a relationship where happiness and holiness are in competition, the smart money is always on God's holiness.

"DOES THIS DRESS MAKE ME LOOK FAT?"

CONVERSATION STARTERS

We've all experienced the frustration and friction that can occur between men and women when they try to have a meaningful conversation (or even just make plans for dinner). God made men and women quite different, but in spite of these design differences, God's plan is that men and women will relate to each other in ways that reveal his glory.

If you are like us, you might be wondering, *Can this ever really happen?* Men and women will never bridge the relational/conversational chasm unless we are able to grasp a deeper level of understanding about what is stirring in the hearts of the other sex.

This part of the book is designed to help you in that quest. Whether you explore these questions on your own, with your significant other, or in a small group, these conversation starters will open the door for you to more deeply examine the themes from this book and help you move past the frustration of feeling hampered by your limitations to a place of more authentic relationship.

BEFORE WE BEGIN

1. What are some reasons you want to read this book?
2. What are you hoping to gain from this book?

GETTING STARTED

1. What confuses you the most about the opposite sex?
2. Men: If you could change one thing about women, what would it be? If you could change one thing about men, what would it be?
3. Women: If you could change one thing about men, what would it be? If you could change one thing about women, what would it be?

CHAPTER 1

1. If you could be any character from a fairy tale, who would you be? Why?
2. Describe your last shopping experience for clothes. How might it have been different if you were accompanied by someone of the same sex? What about someone from the opposite sex?
3. What do you say when asked, "Does this dress make me look fat?" Do you lie, skirt the issue (pun intended), or tell the truth?
4. Men and women both use clothes to define themselves. How does what you wore today define you? What do your clothes say about you? How do you think others read your appearance? Do you even care?

5. How might men and women define *lovely* differently?
6. In what ways can a man call forth a woman's beauty (both inward and outward)?
7. How much has your father or mother influenced the way you feel about the opposite sex?

CHAPTER 2

1. This book addresses several loaded questions that women ask men. Make a list of as many of your own loaded questions as you can.
2. Men are sometimes oblivious (or just pretend to be) to the fact that things they say hurt women's feelings. Let's turn the tables. What could a woman say to a man that would wound or assault his masculinity?
3. Read chapter 2 of the book of Ruth. Notice the way Ruth and Boaz interact. Can you find any similarities between the way Ruth acts and what the authors say about women wanting their actions to be noticed?
4. In your experience, how do men and women create and relate differently?
5. When do you see your wife/girlfriend being creative and revealing beauty? When was the last time you told her or encouraged her?
6. Describe a time when you have been burned by a loaded question. What was the question? How did you respond? What happened?

CHAPTER 3

1. What famous person are you most attracted to? What famous person is your significant other most attracted to?
2. Make a list of all of the cosmetics or other grooming products that you typically use. (Guys, you know you use them too.)
3. Have you ever been busted checking out another person? What was the reaction of the person you were with at the time?
4. What physical thing do you always notice about your significant other? Do you always let him or her know that you notice it?
5. Here is a little quiz: What are your significant other's three most common hairstyles? Describe what he or she wore yesterday. What does this say about how much you notice? Is there room for improvement?

CHAPTER 4

1. What are you thinking about?
2. Make a list of all the things that you would like to do before _____. (e.g., you get married, turn forty, have kids, celebrate your twentieth wedding anniversary . . . you get the idea). Compare these with your significant other's list. How are they alike? How are they different?
3. Right now, ask someone of the opposite sex what he or she is thinking about. See where this conversation goes.
4. Have you ever been asked the above question? What are some of the answers that you gave that didn't work?
5. Have you ever experienced a time when you were in a long-

term relationship and thought about the other person, *You're not quite the person I thought you were*? What was the context?

6. In what relationship do you feel most confident or secure? In what relationship do you feel least confident or secure?

7. In what ways are you looking to your significant other for fulfillment? Where does God fit in?

CHAPTER 5

1. The hand that rocks the cradle rules the world.
   If the momma ain't happy . . . ain't nobody happy.
   Maternity is a matter of fact; paternity is a matter of opinion.
   But seriously, how are you like your mother? How do you think you are different?

2. We all need to grow up a little more.
   a. In what ways do you act childish in your relationships with the opposite sex? Do you whine? Pout? Throw tantrums? Talk baby talk?
   b. In what ways do you treat your significant other like a child?

3. Name a characteristic about your mother that you wish you had. Name one that you hope you do not have.

4. Which mother(s) below most resemble your own? Which mother(s) below most resemble your significant other's mom?

June Cleaver
Martha Stewart
Ivana Trump
The Queen Mum

Mother Teresa
Mother Nature
Marge Simpson

5. What characteristics do you see in a current or previous significant other that remind(ed) you of your mother?

CHAPTER 6

1. Remember playing Duck, Duck, Goose as a kid? What was it like when you weren't chosen?
2. What are the top five things you like about your current or most recent relationship?
3. List five things that you don't like about yourself.
   a. Have your significant other list five things he or she doesn't like about himself or herself. Are there any similarities?
   b. How might these traits affect your relationship?

CHAPTER 7

1. Which couple(s) best reflect your relationship?

Romeo and Juliet
Oprah Winfrey and Stedman Graham
Bill and Hillary Clinton
Kid Rock and Pamela Anderson
Nick Lachey and Jessica Simpson
Elizabeth Taylor and _____ (take your pick)
Fred and Wilma Flintstone
Gomez and Morticia Addams
Dharma and Greg Montgomery

Will Truman and Grace Adler
Ward and June Cleaver

2. When have you slighted (or not chosen) your significant other in favor of something or someone else? What did you choose? What happened?
3. List three areas of growth or change that your significant other needs to address.
   a. Ask your significant other to make the same list about you.
   b. Discuss. Do you agree with each other's lists? How difficult was this conversation? Could you be honest? Were there areas where you held back?
4. The top four areas of conflict for married couples are kids, money, sex, and in-laws. What do you fight about most in your relationship? (Here are some examples: work, quality time, money, social life, finances, relationship with family, relationship with friends.)
5. "God designed relationships between men and women to have more failure than success." In what ways do you agree or disagree with this statement?
6. What myths about your relationship did you believe when your relationship was brand new?

CONCLUSION

1. How has reading this book challenged you? How has it *changed* you?
2. Thinking back to all the *loaded* questions, how would you answer them now?

CHAPTER 1: "DOES THIS DRESS MAKE ME LOOK FAT?"

1. The Weight-Loss Industry: U.S. Food and Drug Administration, FDA/FTC/NAAG Brochure (1992) "The Facts About Weight Loss Products and Programs," presented as a public service by the Federal Trade Commission, Food and Drug Administration, and National Association of Attorneys General.
2. Angela Thomas, *Do You Think I'm Beautiful?* (Nashville: Nelson, 2003), 13.
3. Box Office Analysis, www.dynalivery.com/products/samples/Box.pdf
4. Andrea J. Sedlak and Diane D. Broadhurst, "Executive Summary of the Third National Incidence Study of Child Abuse and Neglect," *Child Welfare Information Gateway*, http://www.childwelfare.gov/pubs/statsinfo/nis3.cfm
5. The Rape, Abuse & Incest National Network (RAINN), http://www.rainn.org/statistics/index.html
6. The Rape, Abuse & Incest National Network (RAINN)

CHAPTER 2: "DO YOU NOTICE ANYTHING DIFFERENT ABOUT THE HOUSE?"

1. Genesis 2:18, NIV
2. Genesis 1:27, NIV

CHAPTER 3: "DO YOU THINK THAT WOMAN IS PRETTY?"

1. "Pots of Promise," *The Economist,* May 22, 2003.
2. Matters of Scale, January/February 1999 Spending Priorities

Sources, UN Development Programme (UNDP), *Human Development Report 1998* (New York: Oxford University Press, 1998), 30–37.

3. Amie Streater, "Fashion retailers set to chase big profits from women over 40," May 17, 2006, Knight Ridder Newspapers. Statistics are for March 2005–February 2006.

4. Anastasia Higginbotham, "Teen Mags: How to Get a Guy, Drop 20 Pounds, and Lose Your Self-Esteem," *Women Images and Realities* (California: Mayfield, 1999): 87–90.

5. See Genesis 2:4-25

CHAPTER 4: "WHAT ARE YOU THINKING ABOUT?"

1. Genesis 3:16, NIV

2. This is not to say that women and men don't have equal standing before God. The Bible is overly clear on this point. See Acts 2:17-18; 1 Corinthians 11:11-12; 1 Corinthians 12:7; Galatians 3:27-28; 1 Peter 4:10.

3. Genesis 3:17-19, NIV

CHAPTER 5: "AM I LIKE MY MOTHER?"

1. Deborah Tannen, *You're Wearing That?: Understanding Mothers and Daughters in Conversation* (New York: Random 2006), 1.

2. Ruth 1:11-13, NIV

3. Ruth 1:16-18, NIV

4. Ruth 1:20-21, NIV

5. Ruth 4:14-15, NIV

CHAPTER 6: "ARE YOU AS HAPPY AS I AM?"

1. "Are We Happy?" Pew Research Center Web site, http://pewresearch.org/social/pack.php?PackID=1 (accessed July 15, 2006).

2. These categories were based on relationship myths discussed by Jeff Helton in a sermon series he presented at Fellowship Bible Church, Brentwood, Tennessee, July 16, 2006, and July 23, 2006. Helton is the coauthor with his wife, Lora, of *Authentic Marriages: How to Connect with Other Couples Through a Marriage Accountability Group* (Chicago: Moody Press, 1999).

3. David Wilcox, *Big Horizon* album released in 1994 on A&M Records. "Break in the Cup" lyrics are the property and copyright of David Wilcox. www.davidwilcox.com.

4. 1 Corinthians 7:1-9, NLT

5. See Ephesians 5:21-33

6. See John 2:1-11

CHAPTER 7: "IS THERE ANYTHING YOU DON'T LIKE ABOUT ME?"

1. Steven C. Clark, Adam M. Dover, Glenn Geher, and Paul K. Presson, "Perceptions of Self and of Ideal Mates: Similarities and Differences across the Sexes." *Current Psychology* 24, no. 3 (Sep 2005): 180–202, 23p, 7 charts.

2. Ephesians 1:4-5, NLT

3. Ephesians 1:9, NLT

4. See Psalm 139

5. Angela Thomas, *Do You Think I'm Beautiful?* (Nashville: Nelson, 2003), 32.

CONCLUSION

1. Stephen James and David Thomas, *Becoming a Dad: A Spiritual Emotional and Practical Guide* (Orlando, Fla.: Relevant Books, 2005), 128.

ABOUT THE AUTHORS

STEPHEN JAMES AND DAVID THOMAS are coauthors of the companion books *"Does This Dress Make Me Look Fat?"* and *"Yup." "Nope." "Maybe."* (Tyndale), as well as *Becoming a Dad: A Spiritual, Emotional and Practical Guide* (Relevant). Stephen and David are regularly featured on radio and television, including ABC Family Channel's *Living the Life,* and in numerous publications, including *Discipleship Journal* and *Relevant* magazine.

Stephen is the congregational-care pastor at Fellowship Bible Church in Brentwood, Tennessee, and a private-practice counselor. He speaks frequently about men's issues, marriage/relationships, and authentic spirituality. Stephen received his master's in counseling from Mars Hill Graduate School at Western Seminary, Seattle. He and his wife, Heather, live in Nashville with their four children.

David is director of counseling for men and boys at Daystar Counseling Ministries in Nashville. He is the coauthor of *Becoming a Dad: A Spiritual, Emotional and Practical Guide.* He and his wife, Connie, have a daughter and twin sons.

New from the authors of
Becoming a Dad

CP0043